AIDS TO MODERN ENGLISH
Diesterwegs Neusprachliche Arbeitsmittel

Englische Nacherzählungstexte für die Mittelstufe

Herausgegeben
von
KONRAD FUCHS

D1673404

VERLAG MORITZ DIESTERWEG
Frankfurt am Main · Berlin · München

4106

ISBN 3-425-04106-1

3. Auflage 1972

Der Nachdruck erfolgt mit Genehmigung des Verlages *Longmans, Green and Co.,
London.*

Gesamtherstellung: Union Druckerei GmbH Stuttgart

INHALTSVERZEICHNIS

EINFÜHRUNG 5

I. ANIMAL STORIES
   1. The Jewel in the Monkey's Heart (circ. 550 words) 7
   2. The Clever One outwitted (circ. 547 words) 9
   3. The Old Stag (circ. 544 words) 11
   4. Pomara, the Sealion's Friend (circ. 533 words) 12
   5. The Kind-Hearted Elephant (circ. 512 words) 14
   6. Down below and up above (circ. 508 words) 16
   7. The Coyote's Story (circ. 507 words) 17
   8. The Strong Ox (circ. 500 words) 19
   9. The Young Bears and their Troubles (circ. 483 words) 21
  10. The Crafty Sprat (circ. 477 words) 22
  11. The Clever Fox (circ. 474 words) 24
  12. The Stork and the Heron (circ. 471 words) 25
  13. The Three Cubs (circ. 470 words) 27
  14. The Biter Bitten (circ. 463 words) 28
  15. Polly flies away from Home (circ. 445 words) 30
  16. The Camel's Story (circ. 437 words) 31
  17. The Blue Jackal (circ. 419 words) 33
  18. The Sparrow and the Weathercock (circ. 414 words) 34
  19. How the Owls of the Pampas treated their Friends (circ. 412 words) 36
  20. For One Day only (circ. 412 words) 37
  21. The Conceited Fly (circ. 396 words) 39
  22. The Clock-Work-Mouse's Tale (circ. 335 words) 40
  23. The Stork (circ. 321 words) 41
  24. Grey Lag the Leader (circ. 316 words) 42

II. JUST SO STORIES — OLD AND NEW
   1. A Lucky Scare or the Story how a Dish came into Existence (circ. 550 words) 44
   2. Federigo's Falcon (circ. 539 words) 46
   3. The Wonderful Ingredient (circ. 520 words) 47
   4. The Hat (circ. 453 words) 49
   5. The King's Pimple (circ. 415 words) 51
   6. The Cat (circ. 396 words) 52
   7. The Old Tin Soldier (circ. 326 words) 53

III. MYSTERIOUS STORIES
   1. How the Tortoise came to have a Shell (circ. 550 words) 55
   2. The Shop on the Beach (circ. 549 words) 57
   3. Limpy Peter's Pet (circ. 546 words) 59

4. Dibble's Garden (circ. 499 words) 61
5. The Swan (circ. 497 words) 62
6. The "Elizabeth Kilner" (circ. 388 words) 64
7. The Cry in the Fog (circ. 332 words) 65

IV. ADVENTUROUS STORIES
1. The Last Dragon (circ. 545 words) 66
2. An Adventure under the Sea (circ. 539 words) 68
3. A Queer Wreck (circ. 431 words) 69
4. The Peewit's Storm (circ. 316 words) 71

QUELLENNACHWEIS 73

EINFÜHRUNG

In zunehmendem Maße wird die Nacherzählung zum Thema der Klassenarbeiten auf der Mittelstufe. Nun stellt gerade diese Stufe besondere Ansprüche an Nacherzählungstexte, da diese einmal vom Schwierigkeitsgrad her betrachtet dem Leistungsstand des Mittelstufenschülers gerecht werden sollen, dann ihn aber auch vom Inhalt her ansprechen müssen, d. h. daß sie ein angemessenes Niveau voraussetzen. Denn Sinn und Zweck einer Nacherzählung soll ja nicht nur sein, die sprachlichen Fähigkeiten zu fördern; sie soll gleichzeitig eine erzieherische Aufgabe erfüllen. Diesen beiden Anforderungen, besonders aber der letzteren, unter entsprechender Berücksichtigung der sprachlichen Voraussetzungen, die auf der Mittelstufe gegeben sind, gerecht zu werden, stellt ein recht kompliziertes Problem dar. —

Um beiden Anforderungen zu genügen, wurden für die Sammlung vor allem solche Texte herangezogen, die vom Inhalt her der Fabel entsprechen, ihr zumindest aber sehr nahe kommen. Der Mittelstufenschüler begegnet in ihr nämlich einer Darstellungsart, die ihm vom Deutschunterricht der Unterstufe bereits vertraut ist, so daß er sich sowohl sprachlich als auch inhaltlich nicht durch sie überfordert sieht, jedoch auch nicht zur Wiedergabe ihm inhaltlich nicht mehr angemessener Texte aufgefordert wird.

Die in den Kapiteln "Just so Stories — Old and New", "Mysterious Stories" und "Adventurous Stories" erscheinenden Texte sind inhaltlich zum größeren Teil einfacherer Art als die des 1. Kapitels. Sie wollen — auch unter sprachlichem Aspekt betrachtet — insbesondere für den Anfang der Mittelstufe als geeignet angesehen werden. Doch wurde auch bei ihnen auf einen angemessenen Inhalt besonderer Wert gelegt, damit sie für den Mittelstufenschüler attraktiv sind.

Der Umfang der aufgenommenen Texte liegt zwischen 316 und 550 Wörtern. Texte dieses Umfangs erschienen für den Mittelstufenschüler weder zu lang noch zu kurz. Schließlich umfaßt die Mittelstufe mehrere Klassen, so daß eine Erhöhung der Anzahl der Wörter nur natürlich erscheint. Mit ihr wurde auch der Schwierigkeitsgrad gesteigert.

Die Kürzungen, die bei sämtlichen Texten erforderlich waren, erfolgten dort, wo die Aussage als nicht wesentlich erschien. Dadurch soll erreicht werden, daß der Schüler nicht durch Unwesentliches vom Wesentlichen bei der Textwiedergabe abgelenkt wird.

Die Worterklärungen am Rande der Texte, die nach Möglichkeit einsprachig gehalten sind, sind in erster Linie zur Angabe für den Schüler gedacht. Es muß natürlich dem Unterrichtenden überlassen bleiben, sie zu ergänzen oder Streichungen vorzunehmen, da aufgrund des Unterstufenunterrichts das eine oder andere am Textrand erklärte Wort bereits bekannt ist, wohingegen als bekannt vorausgesetzte Wörter oder Ausdrücke noch nicht vorgekommen sind.

Von den bereits erwähnten Kürzungen abgesehen, wurde das Original in keinem Fall geändert. Auch hinsichtlich der Rechtschreibung wurde stets in Anlehnung an das Original verfahren.

Der Herausgeber hofft, daß sich die von ihm in die Sammlung gesetzten Erwartungen erfüllen mögen.

Mainz 1966   Dr. Konrad Fuchs

I. ANIMAL STORIES

The Jewel* in the Monkey's Heart

circ. 550 words
* ['dʒuːəl]

On the banks of the River Kistna grew a fine mango[1] tree. Here a monkey made his home. He called himself Moti[2], the Pearl, because his mother had told him that every monkey has in his heart the sweetest jewel in the world, the pearl.

One day Mugger[3], the crocodile, crawled[4] up on the shore to lie under the shade of the mango tree. He saw Moti and called up to him, "Will you be my friend?"

"Yes," said Moti, "I shall be delighted to be your friend."

From that day on every afternoon Mugger came along for a friendly chat.

One day the monkey told the crocodile about the secret place in his heart and what a treasure lay there.

That evening, after he had bade Moti good-bye, the crocodile swam across the river to his home under the other shore. There he gave his wife a mango, a present from Moti. As she ate the mango he told her the story of the monkey's heart.

"I must have that pearl," cried his wife. "Bring the monkey to visit me."

"But the monkey cannot swim. He cannot come to visit us."

"You are a foolish crocodile," scoffed[5] his wife. "Invite him to dine with us to-morrow. Bring him on your back."

At last Mugger agreed, and his wife went peacefully to sleep.

The next morning the crocodile set off to visit his friend.

Moti was delighted to see him again.—"My friend," said the crocodile, "my wife invites you to dinner to-day at five o'clock. Will you come on my back to our home on the opposite shore of the river?"

[1] ['mæŋgou] Indian fruit and tree

[2] [mouti]

[3] ['mʌgə]

[4] krept

[5] mocked

6 talking idly

"Certainly," agreed the monkey.—They spent the morning and early afternoon gossiping[6] together.

"It is four o'clock," said Moti suddenly. "Your wife will be expecting us."

"Jump on my back. Are you comfortable?"—"Your back is quite comfortable," said the monkey as he seated himself. "Let me see how fast you can swim."

Poor monkey!—Suddenly the crocodile raised his head, big tears dripping from his eyes.

"Why do you weep?" asked the astonished monkey. "I weep for you, my friend," answered Mugger mournfully. "My wife will kill you in a few minutes."

"I don't understand you," cried Moti. "Explain yourself."

The crocodile wiped his eyes, and told his friend what was in store for him.

"Listen, Mugger," suddenly shouted Moti. "Why did you not tell me before we started that your wife wanted the pearl in my heart? Unfortunately, I have left my

7 ['preʃəs] valuable
8 uppermost, highest

heart at home. My heart is a precious[7] thing. I do not carry it about with me. I keep it on the topmost[8] branch of my tree."

9 uttered

"Then it is no good my bringing you to my wife," stammered[9] the crocodile.

"Not a bit of good," said the monkey. "But we can go back to the mango tree, and fetch that heart of mine with the pearl. We must please your wife."

Cried Mugger: "Let us go back at once."—With these words he started to return.

They reached the shore, the monkey jumped off the crocodile's back.

When safe he shouted, "Do you think I could live if I left my heart behind? I made up that foolish tale to save my life. You are a fool, and your wife is a monster. Be off!"

(abridged)

The Clever One outwitted*

Long ago, when men and beasts were more friendly than they are now, there lived in a jungle[1] a lion who knew the leaves that were good to eat for this ill and for that. Indeed he was so full of knowledge that he did an excellent trade in herbs[2].

Unfortunately as he grew rich he also grew greedy[3] and vain[4].

One day some people from a distant village begged him to heal their sick. The lion agreed, and packed the herbs he thought he would need in a bundle. Then he looked about for a servant to carry it. Seeing a wild pig he called him, saying: "Will you go a journey with me?"—The pig grunted his consent. The bundle was given him to carry, and the two set out.

When they had gone some distance, the lion stopped before a bush.—"Look," he growled, "that is the medicine to put in porridge. If they make porridge for us at the end of the journey you must get some of these leaves."

"Yes," grunted the pig.

When they reached the village of the sick people a meal of porridge was cooked for them. The lion stroked his whiskers[5]. "Master Pig," he growled, "go and get the leaves I showed you."

The pig ran off to fetch them. Back with them, the greedy lion had finished all the porridge. So Master Pig went to bed hungry.

The next day they returned to the jungle. The pig arrived at his home in a famished[6] condition, to the great sorrow of his wife and children.—"The lion is too clever for us," they grunted.

Not long afterwards, some folk[7] from another village asked the lion to heal their sick. He agreed because he knew he would be well fed.

Again he looked for someone to carry his bundle. This time he spied a rabbit.

"Friend Rabbit," he growled, "will you go on a journey with me?"

circ. 547 words
* overreached, G. überlistet

[1] [ˈdʒʌŋgl]

[2] plants

[3] avaricious

[4] conceited, proud

[5] face-bristles, G. (here) Backenbart

[6] very hungry

[7] people

9

"Certainly," said the rabbit briskly[8].—The lion gave him his load, and they started off.

When they had gone some way, the lion stopped before a bush. "Master Rabbit," he purred[9]. "The leaves on that bush are the medicine for porridge. If they make porridge for us at the village, you must run back and get these leaves. Mixed with porridge they will make you as strong as a lion."

"Certainly," said the rabbit briskly.

They continued their journey. But they had not gone far when bunny[10] suddenly stopped.

"Where is my knife?" he cried. "I must have left it by that bush."—The rabbit ran back, pulled some leaves from the medicine[11] bush, and hid them in the bundle. He soon reached the lion again, and they continued their journey.

In the evening a dish[12] of porridge was cooked for the visitors. The lion stroked his whiskers.

"Master Rabbit," he growled[13], "go and get the leaves I showed you."—The rabbit at once untied the bundle, and produced the leaves.

Now the lion was the vainest of all lions. When he saw the leaves thus produced, he was so angry that he could not eat a bite; and the rabbit had all the porridge to himself.

The lion thought himself very cunning[14] when he deceived poor pig, but he found the rabbit too much for him.

(abridged)

8 lively, quickly

9 vibrating sound expressing pleasure, G. (here) grunzen

10 pet name for rabbit

11 ['medsin]

12 meal

13 murmured

14 sly

10

The Old Stag*

circ. 544 words
* male deer,
G. Hirsch
[1] G. Pirschjäger

Animals have their friends just as we have.—

One evening the head stalker[1] and I were watching the mountain when we saw a large herd of deer coming down from the heights. The country was covered with snow.— They were coming down quickly, heading for the shelter of the big woods.

We knew what this meant. It meant that the night would bring more snow and wild weather, and the deer, able to smell the approaching storm, were leaving the high country for the shelter of the woods.

On their way down the mountain they had to leap the deep bed of a dry stream. In a few minutes the last of them was over, and it was then that we noticed two solitary[2] figures slowly following far behind the rest. Getting my telescope[3] on them, I saw a sick and broken stag, yet round him was running a faithful little hind[4].

[2] lonely
[3] [ˈteliskoup]
[4] female deer

"I'm afraid the poor fellow's seen his last storm," I said to the stalker, as I handed my telescope to him. "He would have given in before this if the young hind hadn't kept him going."

We watched the two coming slowly down after the others, till they reached the deep stream. Eagerly the young hind bounced[5] across, then looked back for her master to follow.

[5] jumped

But he could not do it.

So she came right down the slope till she found a place where a child could have crossed, and this time he dared to follow. Slowly across the ice he went till he gained the centre of the stream; then this legs went from under him, and down he crashed, to lie quite still.

It was a sad spectacle. Could one doubt that the young hind loved him? She stood over him, sniffing his coat, looking this way and that, as though still seeking a way out of the difficulty, but did she know that when a stag falls and gives in, he gives in completely and utterly, and will rarely try to rise?

"A pity to let him die", I pointed out. "Why not get the pony and a rope, and we'll pull him out?"

11

We went. As we drew near, the young hind ran round in a much agitated way. But he merely looked at us in a hopeless sort of way, and even when we went right up to him he made no effort to rise.

We got the rope over him without any trouble and heaved him ashore. We kicked[6] the snow and ice from his shoulders, and leaving him in a sheltered place we spread a hearty meal under his nose, and we went our way. For he made no effort to rise.

Snow fell that night, but it was fine before the dawn, and going up the hill to where we had left the stag, we found that he had eaten his supper, and there in the snow were the marks of his great hoofs leading down to the big wood, while beside them were the smaller impressions of the little hind. So all was well with them, and we knew that it was one of those rare occasions when man can be a real friend to a wild creature.

(abridged)

6 stroked

Pomara,* the Sea-Lion's Friend

circ. 533 words
* [pə'mɑːrə]

The young sea-lions always gather around when the old sea-lion, Greybeard, seemed ready to tell the stories of his adventures.

One summer night the old sea-lion began: "One afternoon, having tired myself with play, I fell fast asleep on a platform of rock. Suddenly I was awakened by something falling over me, and striking me a cruel blow on the nose. I started up with an angry snort[1], and there I saw a poor little girl lying all in a heap."

"A little girl!", asked the sea-lions.—"Her name was Pomara," answered Greybeard. "She was a dear child. I crawled to her, and wondered what was the matter. Pomara was delighted at seeing me so close. She tried to entice[2] me to talk to her. She was not much hurt and was soon able to walk home.

Every day after her accident she used to come down

1 sound made in driving breath out through the nose, G. Schnauben

2 allure, G. verlocken

12

to the shore. She had no one to play with, and she seemed delighted to have found a friend in me.

After she and I became friends, she used to bathe with me," went on Greybeard, "and such a merry time we had together."

"I nearly forgot to tell you," went on Greybeard more cheerfully, "that one of my great pleasures was feeding my little mistress. She was often hungry. I used to dash off through the surf[3], and dart about till I caught some fine fish, which I would take to land and lay at her feet. How her eyes would brighten, and she would rest her head against mine, and pat[4] me and thank me. Then she used to run and light a fire, and heat the food before she ate it.

One day Pomara came to me in great excitement. "I am going away, Greybeard," she cried.

"Going away!" I cried.

"Yes," she answered, beginning to weep, "and I shall not have you to play with, my poor Greybeard. We shall have no more swims or fun together."

"I tried to comfort her. "I wish I could come with you," I murmured.

"I will come to say good-bye to you," she promised.

"That evening to my joy she came again. I scrambled[5] eagerly over to the rocks to meet her."

"I have a grand chance for you, Greybeard," she said, her eyes shining with excitement.

"There is a good white man," went on Pomara, stroking my head. "He told me he wanted to get a young sea-lion to take away over the sea to a place where everyone would admire him. He promised faithfully that you would be very happy. So what do you say?"

"Next morning a party of men, led by Pomara, came to my pool. Pomara called me and I climbed out on the bank. The men took me up and carried me off. They put me on board ship, and gave me a large tank to swim in. They fed me, and petted[6] me all through the voyage. I was sent to the Zoological Gardens, and here I have been ever since.

[3] foam of sea breaking on shore, G. Brandung

[4] strike gently

[5] made my way by clambering, G. klettern

[6] fondled, G. (ver=) hätschelten

I missed the great southern ocean at first," sighed the old sea-lion, "but I have grown used to my life here; and everyone is very kind to me." (abridged)

circ. 512 words

The Kind-Hearted Elephant

[1] [ˈgændʒiːz]

[2] [ˈlælə]

[3] [ˈrændʒi]

One the banks of the River Ganges[1], where grew delicious grass, was a village. In this village lived a poor old woman called Grandmother Lalla[2].

One day a rich man gave her a baby elephant.

Grandmother Lalla took the best of care of her great baby. Soon she became very fond of him because he was no trouble. The old woman called him Ranji[3].

All the children in the village grew to love him. He carried them on his back; they shared their sweets with him. They had many merry games together.

Ranji was a lucky elephant because he never did any work. He ate and slept. He played with the children, and went for walks.

One day Ranji wanted Grandmother to go to woods with him.—"I cannot go, Ranji. I have too much work to do."

[4] woman having control

Then Ranji looked at his mistress[4] and saw that she was growing old and feeble.

"I am young and strong," he thought. "I will see if I cannot find some work to do. If I brought some money home to her, she would not have to work so hard."

Early the next morning, he went down to the river bank. There he found a man who was in trouble. He had a long line of waggons so heavily loaded that the oxen could not draw them through the shallow[5] water.

[5] of little depth, G. seicht

When the man saw Ranji standing at the bank he asked, "Who owns this elephant? I want to hire him to help my oxen pull the waggons across the river."

A child standing near said, "That is Ranji, Grandmother Lalla's elephant."

"Well," replied the man, "I will pay two pieces of

silver for each waggon that this elephant draws across the river."

Ranji was glad to hear this promise. He went into the river and drew one waggon after another across to the other side.

Then he went up to the man for his money.

The man counted out one piece of silver for each waggon. Ranji was wise. When he saw that the man had counted out but one piece of silver for each waggon, instead of two, he sat down in the road and would not let the waggons pass him.

The man tried to get Ranji out of the way, but not one step would he move. He was a strong elephant.

Then the man counted out another piece of silver for each of the waggons. The man put the money in a little bag and tied it round Ranji's neck.

Ranji trumpeted his thanks, and started for home to Grandmother Lalla.

"Oh, Ranji!" she cried, "where have you been? What is in that bag?" She took the bag off his neck.

Ranji told her that he had earned some money for her.

"Ranji," said Grandmother, "what a good elephant you are."

And after that Ranji did all the hard work, and Grandmother Lalla rested. They were both very happy on the banks of the river Ganges where grow delicious grass and herbs[6].

[6] plants, G. Kräuter

(abridged)

Down below and up above

Down at the bottom of the deepest well that ever was lived Mother Frog and her three sons, Toots, Croaker, and Hop.

Up above, in a little white cottage with a thatched[1] roof, lived an old, old man, Granddad Peck, and his little grandson Timmy. Granddad Peck always wore an old straw hat, and as he was grey with age, and his clothes were grey too, Timmy was never quite sure whether his granddad had grown to be like the cottage, or the cottage had grown to be like his granddad.

In the garden round the deep well there were bushes, apple trees, pear trees, and a lovely flower-border.

But down below at the bottom of the well it was a queer world. You would have thought it so dark and wet and cold and cheerless. But Mother Frog and Toots, Croaker, and Hop just thought it was the loveliest place that ever could be.

Mother Frog really and truly thought that the well was the whole great world.

When Timmy up above used to creep to the well and drop a pebble[2] in, and then wait such a long while to hear the splash, Frog would say, "I'm sure someone will be hurt one day. And it's just bound to be Hop. He's never still a moment."

But Hop followed the pebbles right down to the bottom as they sank through the water; and he had even sat upon one for a whole five minutes. And so he would always say, "Don't you be afraid, Mother. Why, they're just nothing. I can push them over and over with my nose."

Three times a day, up above, Granddad Peck would let the great bucket[3] down twice into the well to draw up water. It used to frighten Mother Frog so much that she could hardly speak.

And as it was drawn up again she would give a great sigh and say, "Thank goodness."

One day while Hop was playing, the bucket came down

[1] roof with thatch, G. mit Stroh gedeckt

[2] small water-rounded stone, G. Kiesel(stein)

[3] vessel for carrying or holding water, G. Eimer, Kübel

16

so qietly that as it reached the water it touched him.

And then with a little chuckle he leaped into the bucket and away he went up, up, up.

His mother screamed: "Oh, my darling Hop!" and Toots and Croaker said: "He always said he would do it, Mother."

When the bucket reached the top Hop jumped out, and sat on the edge of the well.

It was so bright there that he could hardly see.

All the birds in the garden were singing gaily, but to Hop it sounded like the noise of thunder.

Oh, how afraid he was! He did not know what to do. And then he saw the bucket going down again. In he leaped[4], and in two minutes he was back again *safe and sound*[5] in his beautiful world that he loved so well.

As his mother hugged[6] him to her heart and kissed him from his nose to his little webbed toes, he said: "Oh, Mother darling, up there it's just, just dreadful."

(abridged)

[4] jumped
[5] free from disease or defects
[6] kept (him) close

The Coyote's* Story

One day a coyote was walking across a valley. When he had crossed the valley he sat down and watched the ravens. They were doing such a curious thing. They were racing their eyes! One raven would settle himself down on the rock and point with his beak straight across the valley to some pinnacle[1] in the cliffs of the opposite mountains. Then he would say, "You see that peak yonder?"[2]

"Yes", croaked[3] his companion.

"Watch my eyes." Then he said to his eyes, "Eyes, see that rock yonder, go round it, my eyes, and come back." He squeezed[4] his eyelids. They went round the rock and came back towards the raven.

The raven looked at his companion. Then he too settled himself on the rock and said, "I can do better than that. My eyes can race yours. Look at that rock away to the

circ. 507 words
* [ˈkɔiout] North American prairie-wolf

[1] summit, top

[2] above there
[3] talked in a hoarse voice

[4] pressed

17

left." Then he began to squeeze his eyelids, saying, "Eyes, go round yonder rock and come back again to me." His eyes fled out of their sockets[5], away across the valley and round the rock he had named.

[5] hollows

The coyote could keep quiet no longer.

"Ravens," he cried. "Ravens, what are you doing?"

"Why, we are racing our eyes," declared the older of the two ravens. "Did you never see anyone race his eyes before?"

"No indeed!" exclaimed the astonished coyote. "Race your eyes! How in the world do you do it?"

"Why, this way," said the younger raven as he settled himself down. "Do you see that tall rock yonder? Well, I say to my eyes, "Tall rock yonder—eyes go round it and return to me."

The eyes slipped out of their sockets.—The raven, holding his head perfectly still, waited for the return of his eyes. As they neared him, he swelled up his neck and the eyes flew into their sockets again. Then the raven turned round and showed his two black eyes as bright and good as ever. "That is how it is done," he laughed.

"I wish I could do it," said the coyote. "Shall I try my eyes?"

"Why, yes, if you like," said the ravens. "Do you really want to try?"

"Indeed I do," replied the coyote.

He settled down, and squeezed his eyelids to force them out of their sockets, but they would not go.

"We will help you," said the ravens. "Just keep still, and we will take them out for you."

[6] repress

"Yes, yes," cried the coyote, unable to restrain[6] his impatience. "Quick! quick! I am ready!"

The ravens picked them out with a skilful twist of their beaks[7] in no time, and sent them flying off over the valley. The coyote in delight waited for his eyes to return.

[7] bills

"Let the foolish coyote go without his eyes," whispered the ravens to each other. "He was very anxious to get rid of them. He must learn not to copy other people. Let him do without his eyes."

18

Whispering and laughing they flew off across the valley, and disappeared over the mountains.　　(abridged)

The Strong Ox

Long ago a man in India owned a very strong ox. But what pleased his master most of all was the great strength of the ox, and his patience and obedience[1]. His master called him Jewel[2] Horn because he was worth many jewels.

One day Mahala[3], for that was the owner's name, went into a village and said to the men there: "I will pay you a thousand pieces of silver if my strong ox cannot draw a line of one hundred waggons. If he draws the waggons you must pay me the silver."

The village folk laughed, and said, "Very well. Bring your ox. We will tie one hundred waggons in a line and see your ox draw them along."

Mahala brought his ox into the village. A crowd collected to see the sight. The hundred waggons were in line, and Jewel Horn, the strong ox, was yoked[4] to the first waggon.

Mahala was so *puffed up*[5] with pride that he began to whip his ox, crying, "Show what you can do, you rascal!"[6]

Now the ox had never been talked to by his master in this way before, so he stood still. Neither the blows nor the hard words made him move.

The village folk laughed and jeered[7]. At last poor Mahala had to pay the thousand pieces of silver. Sadly he walked home leading Jewel Horn. There he threw himself upon his bed and thought: "Why did my strong ox act so? Many a time he has moved even heavier loads."

At last he got up and went about his work. That evening when he went to feed Jewel Horn, the ox turned to him and said, "Why did you whip me to-day? You never whipped me before. Why did you call me 'rascal'? You never called me hard words before. Why did you shame

[1] [əˈbiːdjəns] submission
[2] [ˈdʒuːəl]
[3] [mɑːhələ]

[4] [joukt] a yoke was put upon, G. anjochen, anspannen
[5] G. außer sich
[6] [ˈrɑːskəl] rogue, knave

[7] scoffed, G. spotten

19

me before all the village? Have you not always called me your jewel and your friend?"

Mahala said, "I was so puffed up with pride. I will never treat you badly again. I am sorry I whipped you. Forgive me, Jewel Horn."

"I will," replied Jewel Horn. "To-morrow I will go with you to the village, and pull the one hundred waggons for you. To-morrow you shall gain what you lost to-day."

The next morning when they went into the village, the men laughed at them.

"Have you come back to lose more money?" they said.

Mahala did not mind their laughter.

Again the waggons were placed in a line, and the ox was yoked to the first. A great crowd came to watch. Mahala spoke to his ox.

"Good Jewel Horn, show how strong you are. You are my faithful friend."

At once Jewel Horn began to pull with all his might. The waggons moved on until the last waggon stood where the first had been.

All the village shouted in praise. They paid back the money Mahala had lost, saying: "Your ox is the strongest ox we have ever seen."

And Mahala and Jewel Horn went home very happy.

(abridged)

The Young Bears and their Troubles

circ. 483 words

Many years ago, there lived in a cave¹ a father and mother bear and their two children, Growly² and Furry³.

The two young bears were constantly asking questions. They thought they could do everything as well as their parents, if not better. They wanted to know what life was like away from the cave, and longed to go out to hunt for food for themselves.

Nearly every day they asked this question, "Can we go out and look for food for ourselves?"

Every day the old bears replied, "Patience! Your troubles have yet to come."

"What are troubles?" asked Furry.—"I think troubles are something good to eat," declared Growly. "Father said once that the honey he brought home gave him a great deal of trouble."

"We must find out for certain what troubles are," declared Furry.

Consequently, next day, when the old bears had gone out, Growly said, "Furry, I am going out to look for troubles. Will you come? It is no use our waiting here for them. Father and mother will not bring any home for us, and they will not tell us what they are."

"I will come with you, Growly," said Furry. "I do hope troubles are good to eat."

"If we find honey we may find some troubles too," declared Growly hopefully.

They had not gone far before Growly stopped near a large dead tree, the top of which had been broken off in some storm. "I smell honey!" said he.

"Where?" cried Furry, jumping for joy.

Growly did not answer because he was busy climbing the tree. When he came to the hole at the top, he cried, "here it is." Then he turned round and lowered himself into the hole.

Furry set to work to climb the tree also, but she had not gone far before she heard Growly crying, "I have got them, Furry! I have got them, Furry! And such a num-

¹ underground hollow
² ['grauli]
³ ['fə:ri]

21

4 agitated stir
5 eager climbing

ber!" Then followed a great commotion⁴ and scrambling⁵ the tree.

Furry, greatly excited, climbed up to the hole as fast as she could, and met Growly just coming out.

"What have you got, Growly?" she asked.

"Troubles, troubles! Run home quickly!" he cried. "They are awful," and he pushed his way out of the hole past her, followed by a cloud of bees.

The poor little bears never stopped running until they reached home, where they found their parents anxiously waiting for them.

"Where have you been?" asked their mother.

Growly and Furry eagerly told their adventures.— When they had done their mother said, "All these troubles that have come upon you serve you quite right. You ought to have had patience and waited till I had time to explain to you what troubles were."

"Oh! I was so hurt," cried Growly. "But, mother, were the honey troubles little troubles?"

"Certainly," said his mother; "you have had no great troubles yet."   (abridged)

The Crafty* Sprat**

circ. 477 words
* cunning, sly
** small sea-fish,
G. Sprotte

One fine day, all the fishes in the sea met together to choose a Chief for the next year.

Everyone wanted to be the one chosen, and the noise they made was so alarming that it woke up the Oldest Crab¹ in the sea. He was so old that the fishes thought he had been living for ever; and he was such a lazy old fellow that he spent most of his time asleep.

¹ Krabbe

He certainly did not want to be the Chief himself. He knew he could never keep awake long enough. But when he heard what all the trouble was about he said, Hold your noise. Each of you can tell me why he thinks he should be Chief, and then I'll choose the one I think is the best."

All the fish agreed, and the Shark[2] cried out, "I'm the fiercest and the bravest. I'll lead them to battle Let me be Chief."

"Have me!" cried the Saw-fish[3]. I can knock a hole in a boat."

"What's the good of that!" said a Shrimp,[3a] "Who wants a boat with a hole in it?"

"Why not me?" said the Flying Fish, "I'm a bird as well as a fish."

Just then a great whale[4] came rushing through the water. "What's all this?" he roared. "Choosing a Chief, are you? I'm your Chief because I'm the biggest and the swiftest."

"*Bosh and oysters!*"[5] called out a little Sprat, "I can race you."

The Whale was so astonished that he held his breath so long everyone thought he would burst.

And before he could speak again the Oldest Crab said, "All right, let the Sprat and the Whale swim a race, and the winner shall be Chief."

The Oldest Crab made all the fishes swim off for three miles and then stop. That was to be the winning-post[6]. He then put the Whale and the Sprat in a line and cried out, "One, two, three, *off!*"

Away went the great Whale like fifty express trains.

But the sly little Sprat perched[7] himself on the Whale's tail and held on tight[8].

So great was the speed of the Whale that he churned[9] the sea into foam for twenty miles around.

In two minutes he had reached the winning post, and turned round to see how far the Sprat was behind him.

At once the cunning little Sprat leaped off his tail and cried at the top of his voice, "I've won! I've won! I've won!"

And all the other fishes, who were glad to be able to laugh at the Whale, called out, "*Spratty's won!*"[10]

And so the Sprat became Chief for the year, and during the whole of that time the silly great Whale sulked by himself under an iceberg.   (abridged)

[2] large sea-fish, G. Hai

[3] fish armed with toothed snout

[3a] Garnele

[4] [weil]

[5] foolish talk, nonsense

[6] post marking the end of a racecourse

[7] set
[8] gripping close
[9] shook

[10] Spratty has won

The Clever Fox

Once upon a time there lived a peasant[1] who had such a troublesome cat that no one could live with him. One day the peasant put him into a bag and carried it to a forest. There he opened it, pulled the cat out and said, "You wretched[2] cat, you can live or die in the forest." The cat wandered about until he came to an empty hut. He crawled in through a window, and decided to make it his home. There was plenty of straw for a comfortable bed. When he wanted to eat, he went into the forest where he caught mice and birds. After eating he always went back to his hut.

One day when he was strolling about in the forest a fox met him. She looked at him thinking to herself, "I have lived many years in this forest, but I have never seen such a beast."

She bowed before the cat and said, "Tell me, stranger, by what chance you come here, and by what name I must call you."

The cat said, "I have been sent here to be ruler of this place."

"Oh," said the fox. "I had not heard of your arrival, but come and dine with me. Be my guest."

The cat went home with the fox. The fox entertained the cat with every kind of game. The two got on so well together that they decided to become partners.

The next day the fox went out to get provisions[3] while the cat stayed at home.

As the fox was running through the forest she met a wolf. The wolf said, "I have looked for you everywhere, but could not find you. Where have you been all this time?"

"Have you not heard," asked the fox, of our ruler? He lives with me, and I have to look after him."

"I had not heard," said the wolf in surprise. "How can I get a look at him?"

"See that you get a sheep ready and make him a present. Put the sheep down near our house, and hide *lest he see you*[4]. If he sees you, you will come to grief."

The wolf hurried off to get the sheep.

The wolf brought the sheep and put it down some little distance from the house of the fox. Then the fox hid the wolf.

As the fox and the cat walked out from among the trees, the wolf, wanting to see the new ruler, began to move the leaves to get an opening for his eyes. The cat heard the rustling and, thinking it was a mouse, sprang into the leaves and fastened his claws and teeth upon the wolf's nose.

The wolf jumped up and ran into the forest, in mortal[5] terror of the cat.

The fox and the cat had provision in plenty.

(abridged)

[4] in order that he does not see you

[5] very great

The Stork* and the Heron**

Once upon a time a stork and a heron lived by a broad swamp. One lived on one side of the swamp, and one on the other.

Often in the evening as the stork gazed across the swamp[1], it seemed to him that his life was very sad and lonely. He therefore made up his mind to marry. "I will go," thought he, "and propose to the heron who lives on the other side." Raising himself from the ground, he flew to the heron's house.

"Is heron at home?" he asked when he arrived.

"She is," answered heron.

The stork said:

"Heron, will you marry me?"

"No, I will not marry you. Your legs are too long, your coat is too short, you do not fly as well as I do, and besides, you cannot support me. Be off and don't bother me!"

Salt and bitter as the reply was, the stork had to swallow it and fly away.

circ. 471 words
* tall, stately bird, G. Storch
** long-legged bird, G. Reiher

[1] marsh, bog

25

When he had gone the heron said to herself:

"How can I live here alone? It is a miserable life. I will not endure[2] it any longer. The stork will make a pleasant companion. I will marry the stork."

The next day she flew to the stork's home.

"I have come, stork," she croaked[3], "to tell you that I accept your proposal. I will marry you."

"No, heron, I can get on without you," answered stork, who was still feeling angry. You may marry whoever you please. I will not be your husband."

The heron began to cry. She did not stop crying until she reached her home.

When she had gone, the stork thought:

"What a fool I was not to take heron at her word. A wretched life I have here alone. I will go and marry her."

The next day he flew to the heron's home.

"Heron," he said, "I have made up my mind to marry you. We will have the wedding *right away*[4]."

"No, stork," said heron, who was still hurt and angry, "if you are willing to marry me, I am not willing to marry you. You may go."

The stork flew home in a rage. When he had gone the heron grew vexed with herself and thought:

"What a fool I was to refuse him. How can I live this lonely life? I am a poor, unprotected bird.

The next morning she flew to the stork's home and offered to marry him.

Angry because she had refused him the day before, the stork said, "I will not marry you now. You can marry whoever you like."

But directly the heron had flown away, the stork regretted his words.

To this day they are flying over the swamp offering themselves to each other; and they are no nearer to wedding than when they began.

(abridged)

[2] bear

[3] uttered hoarsely

[4] at once

26

The Three Cubs*

circ. 470 words
* young ones (of wild beasts)

In a part of a forest lived a lion and his wife. The lioness had two cubs, the fattest, prettiest cubs to be found in the jungle. The lion was a good father. Every day he brought home something he had killed, and gave it to the lioness.

But one day he found nothing that would make a good meal for the lioness. As he trotted home, he found a baby jackal[2] on the trail[3]. He pitied it because it was a baby. It had no fear, and ran to meet him. He held it between his teeth, and carefully carried it home, giving it to the lioness alive.

[2] ['dʒækɔːl]
[3] track

"Have you brought any food?" asked the lioness.

"I found nothing to-day except this jackal cub. I did not kill him, for I thought, 'He is a cub like our little cubs.' But suppose[4] you eat him. He will give you strength."

[4] G. wie wär's, wenn wir es täten

"No, no," said the lioness. "I will not kill him because he is a cub like my little cubs. This little creature shall be my third son."

She fed the little jackal cub and made him fat like her own cubs.

Very soon they began to grow out of babyhood, and often went alone into the woods to seek adventures.

One day a wild elephant came into their part of the forest. The two lion cubs, when they saw him bravely sprang at him. But the jackal cub said, "Brothers, that is an elephant, an enemy of our race. Do not go near him." With that the jackal ran home like a coward.

The two young lions that evening laughingly told their parents how their elder brother had behaved.

The jackal was angry when he heard the twin brothers telling about him. He scolded[5] the twins.

[5] rebuked, G. schalten

The lioness, who loved the three cubs, feared a fight. She called the jackal cub aside and gave him good advice. "You must never, never speak so harshly[6]," she said. "Remember, they are your brothers."

[6] roughly

But her patient pleading[7] made him more angry.

[7] appeal

27

"They laugh at me," he howled[8]. "Am I not as brave as they are? Am I not as handsome and as clever? I am certainly going to kill them."

When she heard this, the lioness laughed quietly. She said, "Listen carefully, my dear. You are handsome and clever, but your mother was a jackal. The lion found you one day, and pitied you because you were a baby. He brought you home to me. I pitied you too. I brought you up with my cubs. Now while my twins are still young, and do not know you for a jackal, hurry away. If not, they will one day kill you. It is not you who will kill them."

When the jackal heard this he was frightened, and softly stole away to join his own people.

(abridged)

8 cried

The Biter bitten

circ. 463 words

Once in Jungle-Land[1] a wild dog was trotting along under the tall shadowing trees, feeling in a very bad temper because he had caught nothing for his supper.

Now it happened that a young monkey had climbed down from her tree-house, and was picking up handfuls of dry leaves and throwing them into the air, chattering[2] with joy as they floated away on the breeze[3].

As the cross dog trotted past, a shower of leaves fell over him, getting into his eyes.

When he could see again he glared[4] round him with angry eyes, and seeing the young monkey at her pranks[5] sprang at her and gave her a sharp bite on the leg.

The young monkey set up such a terrific squealing[6] and sobbing that it awoke her mother, who was taking a nap[7] in the tree-top. Chattering with rage, the mother-monkey came tumbling[8] down the tree like a thunderbolt screaming, "Wretch![9] wretch! What have you done to my little one?"

The dog feared she would arouse the whole Jungle

1 land covered with tangled vegetation

2 talking continually
3 gentle wind

4 looked fiercely
5 foolish tricks, escapades
6 shrill crying
7 short sleep, esp. by day
8 turning somersaults, G. purzeln
9 person without conscience or shame

with her clamour, and cried, "Be quiet! I have done nothing at all."

But the young monkey sobbed out, "Oh, mother, he has bitten my leg off."

"How can *you* cure it?" she demanded angrily.

"Listen," replied the dog, "and I will tell you a secret. —Know that the hair of my body is of such great medicinal[10] power, that if but one hair is laid on a wound it will be healed in a single night."

The mother-monkey said, "Give me the hair."

"Let me take it, mother!" screamed the little monkey, dancing with merriment. And when her mother nodded, the young monkey snatched[11] a hair from the wild dog's throat with such force that he yelped[12] with pain.

Strangely enough, in the morning the little one's leg was quite healed.

Now the mother-monkey was a great gossip[13], and she told the story of the wonderful cure to all the animals she met.

And then, every day animals who had been wounded, began to call at his den[14] to beg a hair of the dog to cure their wounds.

The wild dog gave them the hairs they demanded, hoping they would leave him in peace.

But by day and by night the poor wild dog was harassed[15] and worried. But worse than this was the fact that he was losing so many hairs that he was fast becoming bald[16].

And then, one cold day, the poor dog crept out of his den.—Shivering with cold, and mad with shame and anger, the wild dog went to neither I nor any man knows. He never returned to live again amongst the animals of Jungle-Land.

Perhaps he died from cold, or possibly in time he grew a new coat, and lived happily elsewhere.

(abridged)

[10] [me·disinl]

[11] seized quickly

[12] screamed

[13] tattler, G. Klatschbase

[14] beast's lyingplace

[15] worried, troubled

[16] hairless

Polly flies away from Home

[1] bird with hooked bill, G. Papagei

[2] rested

Polly, a parrot[1], flew away from a bungalow in the evening and went a long way. Then it got dark, the rain came, and she did not know the way back. She perched[2] on a big tree. All night it rained, and poor Polly got very wet, and cold, and hungry.

Next morning she saw all the birds flying about, and presently a number of other parrots came and perched on the branches round her. Now the wild parrots are very particular[3] about their dress, and always look clean, well combed[4] and brushed; so when they saw poor wet Polly, they all began screaming and laughing at her.

[3] scrupulous

[4] [koumd]

So Polly got angry, and said, "You are all very rude and unkind. I will not stay with you." She flew down upon the grass, but they came after her, kicking and screaming, and pulling her tail. Presently, however, a large grey hawk[5] came sailing over and they all flew away, while poor Polly ran under a bush. Here she frightened a number of little quails[6]. The mother of the little quails was very angry and called Polly all sorts of bad names.

[5] G. Habicht

[6] bird allied to partridge, G. Wachtel

Polly said, "I am very sorry. Please forgive me, and give me something to eat, for I am hungry."

The old quail, who was a good-natured bird, forgave her and said, "Come along, I will show you something good to eat." She went to an old stump of a tree, and there were a number of ants which she and her little ones began to eat. But Polly did not like ants. She said she was accustomed to have bread and milk.

The quail said, "I cannot help you. Go and ask somebody else."

Polly went down to the river. It was running very fast. The muddy waves came over her, she was carried away by the water and nearly drowned.

The river carried her down some way, but at last she landed on a thing that looked like a dog, half in the water, and half in the mud.

When it grew dark, the rain began again. Polly perched

30

herself on a tree and wished for the morning. She had had no breakfast, no dinner, no supper. "Tomorrow," she said to herself, "I will go back to the bungalow. All the wild birds have such nasty[7] ways, and I do not like them." The next morning Polly started to hunt for the bungalow.

When she saw her master she climbed up on his shoulder, put her beak[8] close to his ear and said, "Polly has seen enough of the wide, wide world. She means to stay in this bungalow for ever and ever."

(abridged)

[7] ['nɑːsti] very dirty

[8] bird's bill

The Camel's Story

circ. 437 words

In a certain city there lived a merchant who had a hundred camels. He loaded them with goods of all kinds, and set out on a long journey.

When he had gone some distance, one of his camels, whose name was Ugly, *fell limp*[1] to the ground. The merchant did not want to delay, so he decided to divide Ugly's pack among the other camels, and go on his way leaving the sick one behind. This was soon done.

When Ugly found himself alone and without his burden, he got to his feet and began to hobble about cropping[2] the grass. Thus in a few days the poor camel regained his strength.

Now in this forest lived a lion whose name was the Mighty One.

One day the lion met the abandoned camel. The lion spoke to the camel: "My good friend, where did you come from?"

The camel told his story and explained why his master had gone away and left him.

As he listened the lion felt sorry for the poor deserted[3] camel. "While you remain in our forest I will protect you," he said.

Ugly grunted his thanks. He was very glad to have a

[1] got lame

[2] grazing

[3] abandoned

31

protector, as he feared the forest folk[4]. He had not been brought up in a forest.

One day the lion fought an elephant, and received a wound from one of his tusks[5]. This meant he had to keep in his cave[6]. As he could not go hunting, he began to suffer from want of food. At last the lion said to Ugly: "Speak, Ugly, are you willing to offer your life to me? Are you my devoted friend?"

"Master," said the camel, bowing low, "I owe you thanks for your kind protection.—I have something of more value to offer you than my body," went on the camel, drawing nearer to the lion. "I will place these leaves I have chewed upon your wound, and to-morrow you will be healed. To hunt food for yourself is better than to kill a loyal friend." As he spoke he placed the healing herbs[7] on the lion's wound.

"I feel better already," purred[8] the lion, closing his eyes.

As the lion waited for the healing herbs to do their work, he felt glad he had not been persuaded to kill someone whom he had promised to protect.

The next day the lion was so much better that he was able to hunt for his own food. Indeed he told the camel that his long rest and fast[9] had done him good. From that time, the Mighty One and Ugly, the camel, lived in friendship together.

(abridged)

The Blue Jackal*

circ. 419 words
* [ˈdʒækɔːl]

There was once a jackal named Fierce-Howl, who lived in a cave[1] not far from a town. One day he went for food into the town after night-fall. There the dogs snapped at him with their sharp teeth, and terrified him with their dreadful barking, so that he stumbled this way and that in his efforts to escape. At last he ran into the house of a dyer[2]. There he tumbled[3] into a great vat[4] of indigo[5], and all the dogs went home.

[1] underground hollow

[2] person producing colour by dyeing, G. Färber
[3] fell
[4] large vessel
[5] colour made of blue powder from some plants

Presently the jackal managed to crawl out of the indigo vat and escape into the forest. The first creatures who caught a glimpse of his blue body cried out, "Who can this be? Never before have we seen an animal with such a coat. We had better flee."

Now Fierce-Howl saw their terror, and called to them, "Come, come, you wild things! Why do you flee in terror at the sight of me? I have been sent to be your king. My name is Fierce-Howl. I will protect you. Live at peace in the forest under my rule."

On hearing this, the lions, tigers, leopards[6], monkeys, rapids, jackals and other creatures all bowed low and said, "Master, tell us our duties. We are willing to serve a good king."

[6] [ˈlepədz]

Thereupon Fierce-Howl set to work to find duties for them all.

Fierce-Howl pleased all the creatures except his own relations, the jackals. These he cuffed[7] and drove away. Perhaps he was afraid they would know him for a jackal.

[7] stroke

Time passed happily and peacefully. One day Fierce-Howl was sitting in his court fanned[8] by his attentive monkeys, when he heard from afar the sound made by a pack[9] of jackals howling. At this he suddenly remembered his kinsfolk[10]. He remembered he was a jackal and not a king.

[8] cooled (with an instrument to agitate the air)
[9] set, G. Meute
[10] blood relations

His eyes filled with tears of joy, he leaped to his feet, and began to howl in a piercing[11] tone. Directly the lions and other beasts heard that howl, they knew he was a jackal.

[11] penetrating, G. durchdringend

3 Modern English (4106)

"A blue jackal!" they cried. "We will not have a blue jackal for our king."

They hunted Fierce-Howl out of his palace, and out of the forest. For the rest of his life he had to live alone, for his own pack would not have him. When he was king he had driven them away. Now it was their turn to chase him out of the forest.

(abridged)

The Sparrow* and the Weathercock**

circ. 414 words
* small bird, G. Sperling
** revolving metal bird showing whence wind blows, G. Wetterhahn
1 rested

He was a very cheeky Sparrow, but then he was very young. In fact, it was his first really long flight by himself.

"Now, don't you go too far," his mother said, as he perched[1] on the edge of the nest ready to start.

"And mind you're not late getting back," said his father.

"All right, Daddy," he said. And off he went. His wings beat the air clumsily at first, and he swayed and almost came to the ground. But presently he was sailing up, up into the air, over the houses and above the tree-tops.

"This is jolly," he said. "I could go on like this for ever and ever."

But he soon began to feel weary, and then he saw the old Weathercock on the top of the church steeple.

2 short sharp note of a sparrow, G. zirpen

3 ['raːskəl]

4 impudent, G. frech

5 trap, G. Attrappe

With a tired chirp[2] he perched himself on the Weathercock's tail.

"Here, you rascal[3]," said the Weathercock, "how dare you sit on my tail? Get off at once."

"Pooh!" replied the cheeky[4] little Sparrow, "I shan't hurt your old tail. You're not a bird at all—you're only a dummy[5]."

"Dummy!" roared the Weathercock, "dummy! Why, I'm the best-known bird for miles around."

"Oh, of course," said the cheeky Sparrow; "but can you fly?"

34

"Who wants to fly?" sneered[6] the Weathercock. "Any duffer[7] can fly. All you can do is to fly up and down, just like a dead leaf. Why, that's just what you *do* look like, a dead leaf." And the Weathercock shook so with laughter that he nearly toppled[8] the Sparrow off his tail.

"Well," said the Sparrow, "I'd rather fly than be stuck up here. That must be why you're so jolly proud, because you're so stuck up.—But you don't know everything, for all that," he went on.

"I know one thing," replied the Weathercock crossly[9].

"What's that?" asked the cheeky Sparrow.

"I know it's going to rain," said the Weathercock, with a sly smile. "And if you'd been watching the way I've been pointing all day you'd have known too. Here come the first drops!"

Down came the rain. But the Sparrow did not wait. Off he flew as fast as he could for home.

But when he reached the nest he was soaked from his beak[10] to his tail.

"You naughty scamp," said his mother.

"You wet rascal!" roared his father. "Off to bed with you!"

(abridged)

[6] mocked
[7] stupid person, G. Dummkopf
[8] caused to fall
[9] angrily
[10] bird's bill, G. Schnabel

circ. 412 words
* night birds of prey,
G. Eule
** ['pæmpəs]

1 [vis'kætʃəz]
burrowing rodent
with valuable fur,
G. Hasenmaus
2 hole excavated by
animals as dwelling,
G. Bau

3 small hill
4 looking with eyes
opening and
shutting, G. blinzeln

5 comfort

6 G. Meerschwein-
chen

How the Owls* of the Pampas** treated their Friends

Long, long ago, there lived in the pampas in South America a great many little animals called viscachas.[1] They were good-natured creatures.

In happy friendship with the viscachas lived the owls. The viscachas were very clever at digging burrows[2] and making nice passages, and they kindly allowed the owls to occupy part of their home. In return for their safe lodgings, the owls helped the viscachas against their enemies, and sometimes kept watch for them outside their burrows.

For some time peace and happiness reigned in the pampas. Then trouble began, and the trouble was caused by a viscacha.—The little creature was vain because of his good looks. The owls who would have turned a deaf ear to an old or ugly viscacha were ready to listen to him.

So he decided to call a meeting of his admirers. On the appointed day he took up his position on a hillock[3] while the owls stood blinking[4] around him and began:

"Friends and brothers, you are shamefully treated. You have as good a right to the burrows as the viscachas. Why should they live in ease[5] and plenty and make you work hard all day? Make them give you the lodgings for nothing, or drive them off the pampas altogether. You must not be slaves. You must do no work."

"We will do no work," cried the owls. "Let us rejoice at our freedom."

Then the meeting broke up.

At first the viscachas laughed at the owls when they refused to keep watch for them. Then they grew angry and said: "Unless you repay us for our trouble in digging these burrows, you must go. You cannot live in our burrows and do no work for us."

The foolish owls refused to work, and refused to leave the burrows, so the viscachas decided to turn them out. They got an army of cavies[6] to help them. These cavies, in their brown and yellow uniforms with white facings, looked very terrifying, and many owls fled away at the sight of them.

No longer does the owl take possession of the burrow dug by the viscachas. Indeed, it has to employ its claws and bill to make a dwelling for itself. The tunnel which is made by the owl is not nearly so deep or so neatly[7] constructed as that which is dug by the viscachas.

On the whole the owls must have been happier and much more comfortable before they quarrelled with the viscachas.

(abridged)

[7] nicely arranged

For One Day only

circ. 412 words

Out of the sheath[1] in which it had floated upon the top of a little stream crept a new-born May-fly.

[1] close-fitting cover, G. Scheide

The sun shone from a blue sky, and the water sparkled like a thousand diamonds.

Birds were singing in the trees and in the low hedges of the fields, and early bees made the air loud with their humming.

It seemed a wonderful world, and as soon as the May-fly had drawn her long legs and wings out of the sheath, she spread her wings to dry in the sun.

Then up into the sunny air soared the May-fly up and away over the fields.

Presently she came to a garden, and rested for a moment upon the low branch of a rose-bush.

Crawling along the ground quite close to her was a Snail. The May-fly had never seen a Snail before, and was filled with wonder.

"Hello," she said, "whatever are you?"

The Snail turned his horns towards her. The voice had startled him; but as soon as he saw who it was, he said, "Pooh, it's only a May-fly."

But the May-fly took no notice of his rudeness.

She wanted to ask him lots of questions, and so she only smiled.

² swelling,
G. Geschwulst

"What's that lump² on your back?" she asked.

"Lump!" replied the Snail. "That's my house."

"Oh, how nice!" said the May-fly. "Is it very heavy?"

"Oh, well, you see," replied the Snail, "it's nothing to me, I'm so strong."

"Can you fly with it?" asked the May-fly.

"Fly!" replied the Snail. "No, of course not; why should I want to fly?"

"Oh, it's simply splendid," said the May-fly.

"Really?" answered the Snail, who was becoming very interested; "well, what is it like?"

But the sun was beginning to sink, and the May-fly said hurriedly, "Oh, I must be going now, but I will meet you here to-morrow; and then we'll have a long talk."

"Very well," replied the Snail; "and mind you're not late. Good-bye."

The next afternoon the Snail came creeping back to the rose-bush. He waited hour after hour, but the May-fly did not return.

He did not know that the May-fly was dead, and so he went on waiting until the sun went down.

³ disdainfully

Then with *a sniff of disgust*³ he drew in his horns and went to sleep, saying as he did so, "That's the worst of those flighty things; they never can keep their word."

(abridged)

The Conceited* Fly

circ. 396 words
* vain, pride in one-self, G. eingebildet

There was once a Fly who not only thought himself the finest and greatest Fly that ever was, but also the finest and most wonderful creature in the air, on the earth, or in the sea.

All day long he flew about in the garden, boasting and bragging.[1]

[1] talk boastfully, G. prahlend

Even the Bees, who are usually good-natured and kind-hearted, could not bear him.

The artful[2] Spiders alone pretented to like him, and one old Spider said, "Splendid and beautiful Fly, you are the King of insects. Come here and let me kiss your hand."

[2] sly, G. schlau, verschlagen

But the Fly, although a boaster, was not such a duffer[3] as that.

[3] stupid person, G. Dummkopf

He boasted and bragged so much, that at last the other Flies began to believe that he really must be better and stronger and cleverer than they were.

They even held a great meeting in the larder[4], and one of them proposed that the boastful Fly should become their King. But a wise old Blue-bottle[5] said slyly, "Perhaps he will tell us a little more of his wonderful deeds first, or he might even show us one or two."

[4] room or cupboard for meat etc.

[5] blowfly, G. Schmeißfliege

"Tell you some more of my deeds!" cried the braggart[6]; "certainly I will. Last Tuesday morning I chased a Lion for five miles, and he only just managed to escape."

[6] boaster, G. Prahler

"Oh!" breathed all the Flies in admiration. "Please go on."

"And on Wednesday," went on the boaster, "I made a Tiger go down on his knees."

"And only yesterday," continued the would-be King, "I flew up after an Eagle, caught him as he reached his nest on a mountain top, and tumbled[7] him down the mountain. I then ate the 325 eggs that were in the nest."

[7] threw

And then the wise old Blue-bottle said, "Ah, yes, but Eagles can look at the sun without blinking. Can you do that?"

"Can I?" roared the boaster. "Of course I can. Come out in the garden and see me do it."

So out into the garden they all flew.

The bragging Fly opened his eyes as wide as possible, and flying upwards stared hard at the sun.

He flew down presently, but the sun's hot glare[8] had dazzled[9] his eyes so that he could not see a bit.

Down he flew—straight into the web of the cunning old Spider. "I *do* love boasters," she said, as she wound him round; "they're so fat."

(abridged)

[8] oppressive light,
G. blendender Glanz
[9] confused the sight by overpowering brightness,
G. geblendet

The Clock-Work-Mouse's Tale

circ. 335 words

It must be very dark in the toy cupboard at night, and how the Clock-work Mouse managed to see it all I really don't know. But he certainly did see it, and this is what he told me:

It was the White Rabbit who began it (said the Clockwork Mouse). The Tin Soldier was telling everyone about the battles he had fought, when the White Rabbit said, "Stuff[1] and nonsense!"

The Tin Soldier turned on him fiercely. "What did you say?" he asked.

"*Stuffing and onions*,"[2] replied the White Rabbit.—"I don't believe you said anything of the kind," replied the Tin Soldier. But as the White Rabbit made no answer he went on with his battle story.

"Fifteen of the enemy were rushing down on me," he said. "What did I do?"

"Cut and run," interrupted the White Rabbit.—What did you say?" asked the Tin Soldier, getting very red.

"*Currant bun*,"[3] answered the White Rabbit. The Tin Soldier sniffed, and, turning his back on the White Rabbit, went on with his tale.

"I was not afraid. Fixing my bayonet[4] in my rifle, I awaited the enemy. They surrounded me. They called on me to surrender[5]. What did I do?"

"Fell on your knees," said the White Rabbit, closing

[1] rubbish talk,
G. (fig.) Kohl

[2] see Nr. 1

[3] bowdlerizing of "cut and run" to annoy the Tin Soldier
[4] ['beiənit]

[5] give oneself up

40

one eye. The Tin Soldier turned pale with rage.—
"*What?*" he roared. "What did he say?—he asked, turning to a Teddy Bear. "He said you climbed up a tree,"
replied the Teddy Bear, hiding a smile.
And with that the Tin Soldier sprang at the White
Rabbit.—The scuffle[6] was dreadful in the darkness. The
wax doll with golden hair screamed and screamed, and
tried to cover her eyes with her little hands.

    [6] struggle, G. Balge-
rei

At last the fighters could fight no more, and they fell
apart still muttering threats.
They were indeed in a terrible plight[7]. The White
Rabbit had lost an ear, his tail, and half the fur from his
back.—The Tin Soldier's helmet was gone, his sword
was broken, and his gun bent in two. And the paint was
all scratched off his face.

    [7] condition, state

Have you ever heard of anything as that?

(abridged)

The Stork*

    circ. 321 words
    * tall, usually white
bird, G. Storch

"I don't believe a word of it," said the old farmyard
rooster[1] crossly.

    [1] the domestic cock,
G. Haushahn

"I don't know anything at all about it," answered the
gander[2]. "What is the tale? If it's the donkey's, I should
like to hear it. It's sure to have a funny end."

    [2] male goose,
G. Gänserich

"Well," said the old cock, "Ned[3] says that last night
a great bird flew over the house. Oh! a perfect monster.
And it dropped right down in front of the farmhouse.
And he said that the farmer must have taken it in, for
he did not see it any more. And now he pretends it will
be turned out here with us, and because it is so big it
will not only eat all our nicest bits, but *us* as well! Did
you ever hear such nonsense in your life?"

    [3] [ned]

The gander turned his head. "Well," he said, "now I
think of it I certainly heard the sound of great wings last
night, and a queer crying noise from over the chimneys."
"Fiddlesticks!"[4] said the old rooster rudely, "you're

    [4] nonsense,
G. dummes Zeug

41

as silly as the donkey. He made it all up to try to frighten us, and as for you—well, you must have had a bad dream from eating too many worms."[5]

Just then the farmhouse dog came by with his tail between his legs, and they all asked him about it.

"Don't talk to me," he said, "I've been worried and chased by everyone in the house. And now they've turned me out. And I've done nothing—this time, anyhow."

At that moment a low wailing[6] cry came from the farmhouse.

The old rooster turned as white as the duck, and the hens shivered with sudden fear.

"Hee-haw!" laughed the donkey, "what have you got to say now?"

But they need not have been so frightened. It was only the new baby that had arrived during the night.

(abridged)

Grey Lag the Leader

There was no sign of danger till the gunshot sounded, when instantly the wild geese rose from the river pasture where they had been feeding. A time or two they circled, looking down at Grey Lag, who had been there leader. His wounded wing had already stiffened.

Earthbound and alone, Grey Lag, who should have been their leader, could only watch them go for the south. Grey Lag was left alone.

Thus Grey Lag attached himself to a little homestead[1], and it seemed that something new was coming into his life—the love of a little girl who fed him! When the time was due for her return from school, he would squat[2] at the gate waiting for her, and when she came, this solitary[3] bird would follow her to the door. From this it was but a step to following her down the road when the school bell rang, and so to the village.

So the days went by, and spring came with its piping, whistling wild bird life in the heavens. Grey Lag felt it, for he spread his sound wing, and day after day he stood on a mound[4] honking[5] and calling and watching the skies. Sometimes he saw other wild geese fly overhead, and they would answer him, and how he would flap[6] and crane[7] his neck as they went across the blue! But always they went on and left him!

But one day he heard an answering honk in the heavens, and looking up he saw a great skim[8] of grey lag geese heading north. The old goose on the grassy mound called and craned and called. The leader in the skies turned in its flight, then down, slowly down, it came within fifty yards; and thither, hurrying as he had never hurried, old Grey Lag made his way. And how they ducked[9] and bowed and chattered to each other!

Grey Lag's mates had come back.

(abridged)

[4] heap of earth, G. Erdwall
[5] crying
[6] flutter
[7] stretch

[8] gliding flight

[9] bobbing (of the head), G. ruckartige Bewegung

circ. 550 words
* sudden fright,
panic, G. Panik
** a particular kind
of food, G. Gericht,
Speise
[1] [ˈeimɔs]
[2] [ˌoubəˈdaiə]

[3] [ˌebiˈniːzə]

[4] [ˈdʒoui]

[5] frog-like animal,
G. Kröte

[6] [ˈkærəlain]

[7] screamed
[8] for keeping various
articles on or in,
G. Gestell
[9] G. Schlagteig

[10] Manscherei

A Lucky Scare* or the Story how a Dish** came into Existence

Once upon a time two little old men, named Amos[1] and Obadiah[2], lived in a small cottage in the country.—And in a very big kennel in the back-garden lived Tim, the dog that folks were warned to beware of.

They had hired a stout boy named Ebenezer[3] to come in each day to clean the cottage and cook their dinner. Now this dinner was a very strange meal, for Amos never dined upon anything else but roast meat, nor Obadiah upon anything but pancakes.

It happened that one day Ebenezer had brought with him his little brother Joey[4], and had told him to play in the garden while the cooking was going on.

Joey had found a spade, and began to dig at the roots of an old tree. His first spadeful uncovered a great hole under a root; and there, sitting at the bottom of the hole, was an enormous toad[5]. He looked so terrifying that Joey dropped the spade, gave a scream of fright, and rushed into the kitchen to tell Ebenezer. It was an unlucky moment. Tim, the dog, sat upon the floor, and Caroline[6], the cat, was stretched out asleep near his feet.

Joey in his hasty entrance trod on Tim's tail. Tim yelped and bit Caroline. Caroline screeched[7] and jumped for the rack[8]. Over went the bowl, and into the baking-tin poured the golden batter[9].

Ebenezer saw the beef floating in the batter. He groaned. "Whatever shall I do?"

At that most dreadful moment Amos and Obadiah entered the kitchen to see how the dinner was progressing. Their eyes fell upon the mess[10] in the baking-pan.

Ebenezer fell upon his knees.

"Masters!" he sobbed, "it was a sorry accident."

"My noble beef!" groaned Amos.

"My princely pancakes!" moaned[11] Obadiah.

"Hullo! hullo!" boomed[12] a voice from the doorway. The newcomer was Matthew[13], the blacksmith from over the way. He said, "It's no use crying over spilt batter; you must make the best of it."

"My beef is ruined," sighed Amos.

"My batter is wrecked," groaned Obadiah.

"Why, stick it in the oven and cook it as it is! It may taste delicious. I'll stay and share it with you."

And so into the oven they popped[14] the baking-tin, with the beef floating in the golden batter.

And after exactly fifteen minutes, Amos and Obadiah and Matthew hurried into the parlour[15], sitting themselves at table.

In came Ebenezer, bearing the baking-tin before him. The batter had risen up into a great golden-brown dome[16], and here and there upon its crust sizzled[17] the juicy chunks[18] of beef.

Five minutes from that moment there was not a morsel[19] left. Amos sat back in his chair and said, "A marvellous dish!"

Obadiah cried, "A luscious[20] cate!"[21]

Matthew roared, "A tit-bit for a potentate!"—They shouted for Ebenezer, and when he came they asked him how the accident had happened. He shook his head and said he did not know. But Joey was listening behind the door, and creeping in cried out in an excited voice, "A toad in a hole frightened me."

Matthew laughed and said, "Toad-in-the-hole would be a fine name for that noble dish, don't you think?"

Amos and Obadiah thought so too.—And Toad-in-the-hole it has been called from that day to this.

(abridged)

11 sound to express grief
12 sounded
13 [ˈmæθjuː]

14 put or push quickly in

15 sitting-room

16 ball
17 sound of frying
18 lumps, G. Klumpen
19 mouthful, bit

20 richly sweet in taste [ˈlʌʃəs]
21 a dainty, G. Lekkerei, Naschwerk

Federigo's Falcon*

Federigo was a knight, well known for his deeds and also extremely rich. He fell in love with a young widow, Monna Giovanna¹, who was both rich and beautiful. It was the custom in those days for a knight to show his love for a lady by giving a great number of feasts in her honour, and this Federigo did in honour of Monna Giovanna. But the lady would not take any notice of Federigo. At last he had given so many feasts, and spent so much money that he had only left a small farm and a falcon which he loved dearly.

So Federigo gave up the life of the town and went to live alone on his farm. Not far from Federigo's farm was the estate where Monna Giovanna was living with her little son. The boy paid many visits to Federigo. He soon became much attached to the falcon.

Now one day the little boy was suddenly taken ill. His mother stayed by his bedside night and day, but in spite of her care he got worse.

"Tell me, dear," she said at last, "isn't there anything I can bring you to make you better?"

"If," he said, "you were to bring me Federigo's falcon, then perhaps I should get well."

So she said: "I will go to-morrow morning and get the falcon for you."

The next morning Monna Giovanna set out to Federigo's farm.

"Federigo," said the lady, "I know I have not treated you very well in the past; I have come to make up for it now. With your permission, I will be your guest at dinner, today."

² room or cupboard
for meat etc.

But when he looked into his larder² there was nothing fit for a noble lady to eat.

As he glanced round the room, his eyes fell upon the falcon that he loved so well. "It is fat," he thought. "It would make a dish for any lady." And *chocking back*³ his tears he seized it, wrung its neck, and set it to roast for dinner.

³ repressing

46

The guest ate it without knowing what kind of bird it was. At last Monna Giovanna decided that it was time to make her plea[4] to Federigo. So she said:

"My little son is extremely ill, and the only thing that is likely to make him better is your beautiful falcon." "Madam," said the young knight. "When I heard that you had honoured my poor farm by coming to dine with me, I was in despair because I had no food good enough to offer you. As I looked round I saw my falcon. I thought that perhaps he might make a dish which I need not be ashamed to set before you."

"How could you do such a thing!" she said. But to herself she said: "How noble of him! Shall I ever forget it?" A few days afterwards her son died. She spent a long time mourning[5] for him.

It was the custom in those days that a childless widow should marry again, so that her estate[6] might come under the control of a man.

"Well, then," she said, "if I must marry again, I shall choose Federigo for my husband. He is the noblest man I know."

And so she did.

(abridged)

[4] presentation of a fact or problem

[5] grieve for the loss of

[6] (landed) property, G. (Land=) Gut

The Wonderful Ingredient*

Once King Gourmet[1] ruled over the pleasant land of Gustaria[2]. He was a man with great love of delicate and delicious foods. He used to say, "A fine soup is earth's greatest gift."

And so he sent his servants all over the world hunting for new recipes[3] for tasty soups. But the result was so often disappointing that at last the King said he would hold a great Soup Competition.

He invited all the greatest cooks of the world to come to his palace, and there in the royal presence to make, each one, the best soup of which he was capable.

circ. 520 words

* part in a mixture, G. Bestandteil
[1] ['guəmei]
[2] [gʌ'stæriə]

[3] ['resipi], G. Rezept

47

Fifty-seven of the world's greatest cooks accepted the invitation of King Gourmet.

When the fifty-seven great cooks of the world had entered the stupendous[4] kitchen, the King made them a little speech of welcome, and the competition began.

When it was over, King Gourmet opened the great note-book of the Lord Chancellor, and was about to read out the marks, and name the winner, when there arose the sound of a shrill angry voice outside the door of the great kitchen.

And into the great kitchen waddled[5] a man.

The King flushed furiously. "Who are you?" he shouted.

"I am Bobbwinckle, the world's greatest cook."

"Well, you're too late," replied King Gourmet.

"Please yourself," squeaked[6] Bobbwinckle, "it's your loss, not mine."

The King stared at him doubtfully and then said, "I'll give you twenty minutes."

"Good: twenty minutes, then."

Bobbwinckle, a minute or two before the time was up, nodded his little head four times, and stood back from the bubbling[7] cauldron[8].

King Gourmet advanced to the fire-place with his golden spoon ready. But Bobbwinckle waved him back. "One moment!" he said, and unscrewed the stopper of a silver bottle, and allowed just three drops of a colourless liquid to fall into the soup. Then, after once more stirring vigorously, he turned to King Gourmet and squeaked proudly, "Now taste!"

The King filled the golden spoon and put it to his lips. He took the soup into his mouth, and turned it about with his tongue and then swallowed it. Immediately such a wonderful smile of delight broke upon his face that all stared at him in amazement. Dropping the golden spoon King Gourmet put his arms around the neck of Bobbwinckle and said, "O, marvel of marvels; *thou art*[9] indeed a magician![10] Kneel down."

And when Bobbwinckle had managed to get down upon

his knees, King Gourmet touched his bald[11] pate[12] with the golden spoon and said, "Rise up, Lord Bobbwinckle, I make you the Royal Cook."

[11] hairless
[12] head

When all the others had departed sadly, King Gourmet took Lord Bobbwinckle by the arm and said, "O, most wonderful one, tell me what was in the little silver bottle." Lord Bobbwinckle giggled. "Not so, your Majesty," he squeaked. "That is my secret; but when I die you shall know."

And when, many years later, Lord Bobbwinckle died, he left an envelope for King Gourmet marked, "The Secret of Bobbwinckle: what the silver bottle contained."

With shaking hands King Gourmet tore open the envelope. Inside was a tiny scrap of paper. Upon it was written one word. That one word was "Water."

(abridged)

The Hat

circ. 453 words

"I won't wear it!" I cried.

"Then you shall not go out with your father at all," replied my mother firmly; "you're a silly boy," she went on, "it's a very nice hat indeed."

"I hate it!" I said miserably.

"Hundreds of boys would be only too glad to wear it," continued[1] my mother.

[1] went on

"Then give it to one of them," I said. "It's like a pudding! No boys wear a silly thing like mine." And bursting into tears I ran up to my bedroom, lay upon the bed and buried my flushed[2], wet face in the pillow[3].

Presently my sobbing ceased[4]; but I still lay there, hating that ugly hat for a long, long while. And then, suddenly, there was a knock at the door, and my father entered.

[2] blushed, G. errötet
[3] cushion
[4] stopped

"Come along," he said, "we are going out."

I jumped from the bed and stood before him, staring at him as if I had never seen him before: Upon his head

49

5 put
6 Talg, here descriptively used = talgig
7 footway
8 plastic (as wax)
9 disappeared
10 entrance-passage of a house

was an enormous pudding, round and white and steaming.

As we passed the great mirror in the hall, I noticed that upon my head was perched[5] a suet[6] pudding, a little smaller than my father's, but just as round and white and steaming. I gasped and opened my mouth to speak; but before I could say a word we were out in the street hurrying hand-in-hand along the pavement[7].

I did not know what to say: surely it couldn't be true. And yet true it was. Every moment now we were passing men and boys, women and girls, and upon the heads of all were puddings of every kind.

Trams passed us, buses swept by, and the drivers, conductors and passengers all wore their puddings as if it were the most ordinary thing in the world: as indeed it must have been, for no one seemed at all surprised. There were even little girls carrying dolls with tiny puddings upon their waxen[8] heads.

That was too much for me. "Oh, father, father!" I cried, "look! look" My father put one hand on my shoulder, and shook me gently. But I continued to call out, and he shook me more and more.

"Wake up!" he said; and suddenly the people, the traffic, the street vanished[9]; and opening my eyes I sat up upon my bed, and saw my father standing over me.

Smiling down at me he said, "Come along, or we'll never get our walk."

As we went through the hall[10] we passed my mother. I did not know what to make of the look in her eyes; and so I said nothing, but I never again saw the hateful hat that had caused the trouble.

(abridged)

The King's Pimple*

circ. 415 words
* small local swelling
of the skin, G. Pickel

Once long ago ruled an extraordinary handsome young King. One morning at breakfast his beautiful young wife exclaimed in horror, "My love, your nose! There is a pimple on it."

The King hastened to a mirror. He regarded the reflection of the royal nose for some moments in horror and disgust. It was indeed true; toward the tip, a little to the right was a pimple. It was in truth but a little one, but there it was, and to the eyes of the King it seemed as big as a balloon[1].

[1] [bə'luːn]

"Send my doctors to me," he groaned.

His fifty-two doctors *filed in*[2] one by one, examined the disgraced nose and then stared at one another.

[2] marched in one behind another

And then the unhappy King had to listen to fifty-two different cures[3].

[3] courses of treatment, G. Heilverfahren

The King dismissed them from his presence, and for the next few weeks he tried all the remedies[4] in turn, but without any success. The pimple grew no larger, but it remained visible.

[4] see Nr. 3

And now some of the most discerning[5] amongst the King's courtiers began to notice that the pimple (or "button" as they called it) really improved the King's appearance. They said that before his face had been too symmetrical[6], too perfect, and now the button lent a sort of distinction to the royal mien[7]. They would greet him in the throne-room after breakfast with such courtly phrases as, "The royal button looks charming this morning, your Majesty," or "How delightfully your button looks to-day, O King."

[5] distinguished

[6] [si'metrikəl]
[7] [miːn] look

And then many of the courtiers had little pimples made of wax which—with the King's permission—they stuck upon their noses, but always on the left side of their tips: for it was felt that the right side should be reserved for the King's closest friends. The Lord High Counsellor founded a Button Club, to which only the most distinguished might belong. And very soon membership of this splendid Club became an honour more sought after than any other in the land.

51

Presently the poets began to write poems about the King's button.

Artits too turned their attention to the King's button, and many wonderful pictures were painted of it.

The tradesmen took it up. The gold-and silversmiths made brooches, necklaces, rings and bracelets[8] with the splendid pimple in diamonds upon them. There were King's Button hats, King's Button boots, King's Button cutlery[9] and King's Button everything you can possibly think of; even the toy-shops had King's Button dolls and soldiers and stuffed dogs, cats and rabbits.

(abridged)

The Cat

"The Captain of the *Emily*", said George, "was a gruff[1] old Scotsman named Buchan[2]. When off his ship he lived in London with his wife. They'd no children and the old lady was daft[3] about cats. I believe she'd a dozen of them, and every voyage Captain Buchan would keep his eye open at any port of call for the chance to pick up fresh specimen[4].

"Well, he got a beauty one voyage just before we left New York for home. It was a fine black Tom[5]. The captain named it Tinker, and said his wife would cry with joy when she saw it. Some of us nearly cried with rage before long, for Tinker was about as good-tempered as a bear with toothache.

"Things would not have been so unbearable if it had not been for Gracie, old Sam Dunstan's parrot[6]. Gracie and Tinker were sworn enemies from the first; and very soon Gracie learned to imitate Tinker's mewing[7] and nearly drove the black cat frantic.

"And then one day Tinker sprang at Gracie and seized her. With a roar of rage old Sam Dunstan grabbed Tinker, tore it off Gracie, and then before anyone could stop him had flung Tinker overboard.

"Here was a pretty pickle[8]. I dared not tell Captain Buchan, for I feared his temper. Luckily the weather was so bad that the captain was too busy to think about Tinker; and as Gracie (who had not been much hurt) spent half the day mewing and yowling[9] joyously, the skipper[10] never guessed what had happened.

"And when we put in at Falmouth[11] for a couple of days I slipped ashore and stole the first fine black cat I saw.

"Two evenings later we dropped anchor in the Pool of London; and after we'd been paid off the captain went off home with Tinker (as he thought) under his arm.

"It was over three months before we were off again.

"The first thing I did when I came aboard was to ask Captain Buchan if Tinker was quite well.

"Oh, very well indeed, George," he said; "and only last Thursday she had five kittens!"[12]

"Well, I had to own up then! but luckily the captain treated it as a fine joke. When he'd done laughing, all he said was, 'Don't forget, George, that *all* black cats are not Tom-cats.'"

(abridged)

[8] awkward state, G. mißliche Lage

[9] [jauliŋ]
[10] captain
[11] [ˈfælməθ]

[12] young of a cat

The Old Tin Soldier

circ. 326 words

Once, in his young days, he had been a fine and splendid figure.

At least six inches tall, in his bright red coat, blue trousers, polished boots and shining sword and gun, he had been the proudest of all the toys in the window of the toyshop.

But there he had stayed day after day and week after week, until the months became years, yet no one seemed to want him.

He thought to himself: "If only one would take me, and hold me, and kiss me just *once*, I should be so happy. And even if then I were thrown away I would not care."

But it seemed as if his dream would never come true.

And now the shopkeeper began to get a little cross because the Tin Soldier would not sell.

He lowered the price on the ticket from two-and-six to one-and-six, and then to a shilling. But no one wanted the Tin Soldier, even for a shilling.

Then he was marked at sixpence, and next at three-pence.

And then there came to the shelf[1] a most beautiful doll with golden hair, blue eyes, and a long white dress of silk[2].

After a while, she began to talk with a few of them.

And then one morning he spoke to her.

She just looked at him out of her beautiful blue eyes, and then, turning her back upon him, said something.

There was a shout of laughter from all the toys.

The Tin Soldier shrank back into his corner. His head dropped forward upon his faded and dusty tunic[3]. He did not care what happened now.

The next morning the shopkeeper placed a penny ticket upon him and put him in the *odds and ends*[4] box.

And so if you should come across a battered[5] old Tin Soldier marked at a penny, please buy him before his heart quite breaks.

(abridged)

[1] board, G. Regal

[2] silk cloth, G. Seide

[3] military coat, G. Waffenrock

[4] oddments, G. Abfälle

[5] knocked and broken, G. verbeult

III. MYSTERIOUS STORIES

How the Tortoise* came to have a Shell

circ. 550 words
* four-legged raptile enclosed in a horny shell

Many years ago in the far-away land of Syria there were no bakers' shops. Each mother did the baking for her family. Bread, figs and olives[1] were the food of the children, but bread was the greatest of these.

[1] ['ɔlivz]

The mothers baked it in the ovens[2] that stood beside the village houses.

[2] ['ʌvnz]

One morning two old women decided to bake. The one whose grandson was a sherpherd mixed flour into dough and laid it inside her warm oven to bake. The little old woman who lived alone mixed flour into dough and laid her loaf inside her warm oven to bake.

Presently the loaves were baked. The little old woman who lived alone carried hers into her house where she hid it.

The little old woman whose grandson was a shepherd set her basket on her head. In the basket she had a skein[3] of wool which she had spun. This she was going to sell. She also put her loaf of bread in her basket. She had a long way to go, and she might be hungry.

[3] [skein] bundle

The little old woman reached the market in good time, and sold her skein of wool. On the way home she felt hungry, so sitting down by the roadside she broke her loaf of bread in half. Just as she was about to eat, a blind beggar came along and asked for alms[4]. The little old woman gave the beggar the half she was going to eat, and started on her way again.

[4] [ɑːmz]

She had not gone far along the road when she again felt tired and hungry. She stopped to eat. Just as she was about to begin, a poor hungry child ran up to her asking for bread. The little old woman gave him all she had, and started once more towards home.

She must be quick and bake some more bread for her grandson, the shepherd boy. But she found her oven was cold because her fire had burned itself out while she was away.

"Never mind," she said to herself, "I have a neighbour who baked this morning. She will share her bread with me."

So she ran to her neighbour saying, "A half of your loaf, kind neighbour, and I will bake for you in the morning. I want to prepare supper for my grandson."

The other little old woman was out in her garden. She pretended[5] that she did not hear. She turned her back upon her neighbour.

[5] professed falsely, G. heuchelte

"A quarter of a loaf?" begged the little old woman who had given away her bread. Still her neighbour would not speak or turn.

Suddenly a strange thing happened. The selfish little old woman's oven rose and hung over her in the air like a heavy cloud. It settled down upon her and covered her, all but her hands, feet and her little face and head. She could not free herself. The oven was so heavy that she had to crawl slowly as she still crawls to this day, for she was the mother of all the tortoises.

Look at the markings on the shell of the tortoise, and you will see the bricks of the old woman's oven. Watch for that odd[6] little face peering[7] out from under the shell, and then drawn quickly back in shame.

[6] strange
[7] looking narrowly

(abridged)

The Shop on the Beach

About eighty years ago a stranger came to live at Soleby[1]. He bought a little cottage on the cliffs and there he lived alone.

[1] [ˈsoulbi]

When he had been living at Soleby about two years he bought a plot of land on the foreshore[2] between the cliffs and the tide-mark. To the surprise and amusement of Soleby he set to digging upon his plot of land on the beach.

[2] shore between high and low water marks

One morning while he was at his digging, a fisherman stopped to watch him. By this time the folk of Soleby had made up their minds that Mr. Egerton[3] (for that was his name) was mad, and so the fisherman thought it a good chance to be funny.

[3] [ˈedʒətn]

"Digging for worms, Mr. Egerton?" asked the fisherman.

Egerton stopped digging for a moment. "I'm digging for money," he said.

A few weeks afterward loads of building material were dumped[4] upon the beach by Egerton's plot.

[4] thrown

And when it was seen that he was going to build, the folk of Soleby were quite *sure* that he was mad.

And then one day Parson Sutton[5] stopped Egerton in the street and asked him point-blank what he was doing.

[5] [ˈsʌtn]

"Building," replied Egerton.

"I can see that," went on Parson Sutton; "but may I ask *what* you are building?"

"A boat-building shop," answered Egerton.

"Do you see that greenish line there, Mr. Egerton?" asked Parson Sutton. "That was where the sea came during the last storm-tide, three years ago. If your shop had been here then it would have been washed away by the great seas."

Egerton shrugged his shoulders. "*If,*" he said mockingly, "but it was not."

Parson Sutton turned and stalked[6] away without replying.

[6] walked away with slow strides

Egerton's first boat was built by the middle of August.

[7] [ˈdʌnidʒ]
[8] [riˈgætə]

It was a fishing-boat, and certainly a beauty. He sold it to a fisherman living at Dunwich[7], about six miles along the coast. And at the regatta[8] held at the end of August the new boat left all the others behind.

The years went on. Boat after boat Egerton built in the shop on the beach, and the fame of them spread the length of the whole coast.

[9] rolled

And ever and again storm-tides visited Soleby, and the seas swirled[9] round the shop. But always the shop was unharmed, so that in time the folk of Soleby ceased to marvel at the miracle.

Fifty years passed, and now Egerton was an old man.

And then, two days after Christmas, when he was eighty-seven, he was taken ill and had to remain in his bed.

That night the wind rose and brought once again a storm-tide to Soleby. It was the worst night that the oldest men of Soleby had ever known. And in the morning, where the famous shop had stood, there was nothing but a clutter[10] of bricks, mortar[11], tiles and shattered planks and beams[12].

[10] untidy state
[11] mixture of lime, water etc. used in building, G. Mörtel
[12] long pieces of timber, G. Balken

Half the folk of Soleby, with Parson Sutton at their head, came up from the ruin on the beach to Egerton's little cottage. But when Parson Sutton entered the tiny bedroom, he found old Egerton, lying very still in his bed. There was a half-smile on the dead man's lips, as if his last thought had been a merry one.

If you don't call *that* tale a bit of a miracle, I don't know what you would call it.

(abridged)

Limpy* Peters's Pet

circ. 548 words
* with limping gait

"There's a lovely bird out there in the bay," I said to George. "Aye," smiled George; "that's a cormorant[1]; and if you had a gun and shot it the Government would give you a shilling." "I couldn't be so cruel!" I cried indignantly.

[1] greedy sea-bird

"Well," went on George, "cormorants are terrors for fish. Most every time that chap out there dives he gets a fish, and during one day he'll eat as many as sixty or seventy. And that's bad for the fishermen."

"Oh!" I cried, "it can't be true!"

"True enough!" chuckled[2] George; "and I once knew a comorant that would catch over two hundred in a day —if you'd care to hear the story."

[2] laughed

"Yes, please," I said.

"There used to live about here," went on George, "a little old man called Limpy Peters. He had a game[2a] leg and walked with a limp. He lived all alone in a cottage. He'd a small dinghy[3] and a garden, and by growing all his own vegetables and doing a bit with his nets he managed to *jog along*[4].

[2a] (sl.) for lame

[3] also dingey, a small boat

[4] to get along, G. sein Auskommen finden

"Well, one summer morning, when Limpy was out in the bay, he found a cormorant floating on top of the water. The poor wretch had got its wings mired[5] and mucked[6] with oil from the ships. It couldn't dive and it couldn't fly, and there it would have to stay till it died.

[5] muddied

[6] see Nr. 5

"Limpy was a soft-hearted old chap, and he fished the cormorant out of the water and took it home with him and cleaned it with paraffin[7]. And when it was clean he fed it with live fish.

[7] ['pærəfin]

"In a couple of days it was as well as ever. Limpy took it out to sea and let it go. The cormorant settled on the water near the boat, dived, came up with a fish in its beak, and then flying on to the gunwale[8] of the boat dropped the fish at Limpy's feet. Sounds like a fairy-tale, but it's true.

[8] upper edge of a ship's or boat's side G. Schandeck

"And after that Limpy and the cormorant lived together in the cottage and were like brothers.

[9] anchored chains,
G. Vertäuungen
[10] G. Kleinholz

"And then trouble came to Limpy. A sudden, unexpected storm blew up in the middle of May, and Limpy's dinghy was torn from its moorings[9] and smashed to matchwood[10] on the rocks.

"It looked like the workhouse for Limpy. But a miracle happened, or something very like one. Every day Limpy used to take the cormorant down to the shore and let it go. And in five minutes or so that blessed bird would be back with a fine fish. Hour after hour they would keep it up, and some days the cormorant would bring ashore two hundred. I've known days when the fishermen in their boats were getting nothing and Limpy would have

[11] here : twenty; 5 or
6 score = between
100 and 120

five or six score[11] to sell.

"They lived happily together until Limpy died. And when he was dead Limpy's neighbour, a foxy old man named Joe Towl, said that Limpy had left the bird to him.

"So Joe took the cormorant and promised himself a

[12] free from trouble

nice life of ease[12] for the rest of his days.

"But Joe didn't reckon with the cormorant's plans. And the first time Joe took the bird to the beach and released it, the cormorant flew out to sea and dived. Joe waited and waited; but neither he nor anyone else ever saw the cormorant again."

(abridged)

Dibble's Garden

"Well," laughed George, "it all happened at Soleby, and the tale was told to me, when I lived there, by an old fellow."

"Soleby suffered from what is called coast-erosion[1], which means that the sea eats into the land slowly and surely, so that what once was dry land becomes covered by the sea."

"Now there came long ago to live in Soleby a young man named Dibble. He had laid out a garden quite near the sea. It was a flower, fruit and vegetable garden."

"When Dibble first planned his garden, and began to make it, several of the old fishermen came to him and warned him that it was a silly place to put a garden."

"The sea hereabouts[2] is always hungry, and it eats into the land a few feet one year and a few feet the next, slowly, but surely."

"Pooh![3] a few feet!" replied Dibble. "Well, even if it's true, what you say, there are three feet to a yard, and I'm thirty yards away, so the sea won't worry me in my lifetime."

"But Dibble was wrong. The following winter there was a great storm-tide. The sea came rushing in, snapping[4] at the land like a hungry wolf. And the next day Dibble's garden was gone. With the passing of the storm-tide the sea did not draw back, but remained."

"Dibble was beside himself with anger. He clenched his fist at the sea and shouted, 'Curse the sea! it will go back!' "

"The years passed—five, ten, twenty, thirty, and still the sea covered Dibble's garden."

"He was now an old man, grey and a little bent."

"Another fifteen years fled away. But for all his ninety he was as fierce as ever. And whenever anyone spoke to him of his garden, he would roar, 'The sea'll go back, and I'll wait for it if I wait a hundred years!' "

"And at last the miracle began to happen: All about Soleby the sea began to go back. And round by Dibble's

[1] [iˈrouʒən]

[2] near here

[3] [puː]

[4] biting suddenly

61

garden it went back not in feet and inches, but in great strides[5], so that by the time Dibble was ninety-three, there again was his garden!"

"You would not have known it for a garden; it was just a waste of sand and pebbles[6] and weed[7]. But, old man as he was, he set to work."

"Before he was ninety-seven his garden was as fine as ever. And on his ninety-seventh birthday he invited to dinner at his cottage the only six old men of Soleby who remembered his garden as it had been over fifty years before."

"And he chuckled[8] and said, 'I knew! I said I'd wait. All things come to those who wait.'"

"If ever you go to Soleby, ask anyone there to show you Dibble's Garden. They'll be glad to point it out to you, and to tell you the story too, if you should care to hear it again."

(abridged)

circ. 497 words

The Swan

I had gone with George looking for *bait-worms*[1] by the mouth of the little river. Presently George began:

"It was the spring before the last that young Denton brought his motor-yacht[2] down here and anchored it in the river. For days on end he'd go roaring down the river to the sea where the breakers begin, and then come roaring back again.

He lived all alone aboard his motor-yacht, the I*ris*[3].—In September, two swans came. The very morning after they'd come I saw young Denton standing on the deck of the Iris staring at them. I'd a job down here at the time building a dinghy[4] with Joe Collins.

About half an hour afterward his speed-boat tore down the river to the sea.—About an hour later we saw something: There was young Denton in his racer trying to run down the swans, twisting and turning after them as

Side notes:

[5] long steps

[6] small water-rounded stones
[7] wild herb

[8] laughed

[1] food to entice prey, G. Köder

[2] [jɔt]

[3] [ˈaiəris]

[4] also dingey, a small boat

they dodged[5] here and there to escape him. Before we came up to him he had hit the hen-bird, and she'd gone down under him in *a crumple of wings*[6]. And then he heard us coming. He looked at us over his shoulder, scowled[7], and sitting down hurriedly started the engine and shot off down to the sea.

Th dead swan floated on top of the water, and presently its mate came swimming. It swam round and round the broken body of the hen, every now and then touching it with its beak, and laying its long neck over it.

After a while Joe Collins and I went back to our work. But that evening we called at Squire's[8] place and told him all about it. Squire was furious, and said he'd thrash the young pup. Well, there wasn't any thrashing, but there was a court case, and Joe and I were called as witnesses. Young Denton swore it was an accident; he had a big lawyer down to defend him, and it all *fizzled out*[9].

"What a shame!" I said.

"Wait a while," smiled George, "*the tale's not done yet*[10]."

"Not three weeks afterward," went on George, young Denton was missing; and the day afterward we dragged[11] the river and his body was found.

There was a queer mark on the back of his head. Joe Collins, who saw the mark, said that if it wasn't the mark of a swan's beak he'd eat his hat.

But that wasn't all. The ferryman's[12] wife, who lay awake in pain that night, told that she'd heard a cry over the water just after midnight; and then, a minute or so later, she'd heard the noise of great wings go flapping over the cottage. And, well, that's all!"

"But—but—" I was beginning, when George interrupted me and said, "Now it's no use asking me questions, for I know no more than I've told you."

I set off homeward beside George, wondering a good deal, but saying nothing.

(abridged)

[5] eluded, G. auswichen
[6] wings crushed together
[7] looked gloomily
[8] local judge
[9] was a failure
[10] the tale has not yet finished
[11] here : searched
[12] one who ferries passengers, G. Fährmann

63

The "Elizabeth Kilner"

"When I gave up the sea I spent three years at Soleby, a small fishing-port on the east coast."

"I shared a fishing-boat with Joe and Tom, and the first two years we did pretty well. Our boat was the 'Mary'. She looked clumsy enough, and the children called her the 'Aunt Mary', but she was fast, and, what was more, safe."

"Well, my third year at Soleby the fishing failed altogether."

"There were bad times for everyone early that winter. December came in with an icy north wind, and by mid-December the snow lay knee-deep everywhere."

"And nearly everyone was hungry and, what was worse, cold. No one could afford coal, and although men, women and children scoured[1] the country-side for wood, and combed[2] the beaches for miles for driftwood, no one had enough firing to warm a dog's nose."

"Christmas was only about ten days off, and the children were feeling pretty miserable. Christmas was coming, and, as far as they could see, for the first time in their lives it would be a Christmas with no turkey, plum-pudding or *mince-pies*[3]; and *into the bargain*[4] there would be empty stockings on Christmas morning. They would be lucky, they knew, if there were enough bread."

"Well, on the night of December the sixteenth the wind veered[5] round to north-east, roaring and howling[6] like a hundred mad lions."

"By daybreak, so quickly did the wind drop, that there was hardly a stir in the air."

"And then, as the daylight spread, there was a sight for the eyes of Soleby to wonder at. Two hundred yards north of the coast-guard station there lay, leaning over a bit on her side, a great four-masted schooner[7]."

"Men, women and children went running down."

"The ship—her name was the 'Elizabeth Kilner'—was of no use except to be broken up. A firm of ship-breakers bought her, and all the men at Soleby had the job of

[1] searched
[2] [koumd]

[3] pies of cut meat
[4] over and above, G. obendrein

[5] turned
[6] roaring

[7] ['skuːnə]

64

breaking her up and loading up the wood. The work had to be done quickly for the buyers feared a storm-tide might take her out to sea. Everyone therefore worked overtime with double pay for a whole week. And so there was not a family in Soleby that didn't get its turkey, plum-pudding and mince-pies, nor a child that didn't get its stockings filled."

(abridged)

The Cry in the Fog
(Sailor's Yarn)

circ. 332 words

"Not much of a day this, is it?" said George, as he looked over to the fog rolling in from the sea.

"I don't mind," I replied; "I rather like a fog for a change; it's exciting."

"I'd sooner see any weather than fog," went on George. "My father had a queer adventure once in a thick fog, and I'll tell you the tale if you've the time to listen to it."

"I've always the time for stories," I said.

"Well," continued George, "my father was a sailor, just as I've been.—They were homeward bound one January when they ran into a fog that was about as thick and heavy as a Shetland blanket."

"By nightfall they were fog-bound[1].—When my father came up on deck about four or so in the morning somewhere out in the still, pitchy[2] blackness there sounded a wailing[3] cry."

"A dozen times and more before the dawn my father heard that cry. With the dawn came a breeze; the fog blew away, and the sun showed red over the bow[3] horizon."

"And then, not a biscuit-toss[4] away from the ship, my father saw a dark object in the water. Without stopping to think my father plunged[5] overboard."

"There was a cry of 'Man overboard!' a boat was manned and lowered; and when they reached my father

[1] wrapped up (encircled) by fog

[2] G. pechartig

[3] lamenting, G. (weh) klagen

[3] [bau] bending

[4] very short distance

[5] threw himself

65

⁶ framework of bars,
G. Gitter
⁷ opening, G. Luke

he was holding on to the floating grating⁶ of a hatchway⁷ with one hand, and with the other was fumbling at a shawl. And in the shawl was ———"

"A baby!" I interrupted with a shout.

"Right you are!" laughed George; "and all alive, crowing and kicking that baby was. And to cut a long story short," he ended with a chuckle⁸, "my father took the baby home with him, brought him up, and here he stands before you!" And with a great laugh George struck himself upon the chest and threw out his arms.

⁸ laugh

(abridged)

IV. ADVENTUROUS STORIES

The Last Dragon

circ. 545 words

Hidden upon the top of a steep mountain, the last dragon in all the world stirred¹ in his sleep. Presently he yawned and opened his eyes.

¹ moved

His sleep had lasted for ten thousand years; but this he did not know. He only knew that within him gnawed² a mighty hunger. As he lay there, the memories of plump juicy³ men and fat little boys and girls moved in his sluggish⁴ brain. He licked his hungry lips, rolled himself upon his great feet, and presently waddled⁵ and wallowed⁶ his way out into the sunshine.

² nibbled, G. nagte

³ succulent,
G. saftig
⁴ slowly-moving
⁵ walked with slow
rocking gait,
G. wackeln
⁶ rolled, G. wälzte
⁷ looked narrowly

He peered⁷ down the mountain side at the great city that lay below him in the valley.

Presently, when he was able to look longer, he could see the streets alive with hurrying folk—men, women and children.

As he approached the city, the old memories of the wonderful feasts he had had long ago awoke in his sleepy brain. He remembered with joy his deeds in great cities, the terror of the people, the shouts, the cries and groans,

66

the trampling of running feet, and the crunch[8] of his mighty jaws as he *gobbled down*[9] the lickless fugitives[10].

And having just reached the first street of the great city, he opened his gigantic mouth and let out a roar that shook the houses.

The busy noises of the street ceased like magic. Everyone stared at the mighty dragon. Not a man, woman or child stirred: and then a great shout of laughter went singing up to the roofs of the houses, and a swift rolling cheer burst from a hundred children's throat.

Men, women and children came pouring towards the amazed dragon. They surrounded him, crying, "Hurray![11] a circus!"

The last of all the dragons stared at them with puzzled eyes. A little boy ran under his great nose, and pointing up the street to the city square, cried, "This way, dragon, this way!"

The crowd took up the boy's cry. "This way, old fellow," they shouted.

A pang of hunger gnawed at him, and sudden rage surged[12] into his heart. He would show these people the sort of fellow he really was. And opening his mighty mouth he roared seven times.

But the people had heard enough of his roaring. A dozen voices shouted at him, "Is that all you can do? Pooh! You're only half a dragon."

The last of all the dragons remembered suddenly his most frightful feat.[13] He would scare[14] them now! Once more the great jaws fell apart and out of that vast mouth shot smoke and tongues of fire.

The people cheered a little. "Not bad," cried an old woman, "but my chimney smokes more than that."

But they soon tired and began to drift away.

A great sob broke from the dragon's throat. He raised himself painfully upon his immense legs, and turning, proceeded painfully along the way he had come.

He came again to the mountain, and slowly and sorrowfully he climbed its steep sides. And then, suddenly, the memory of his former greatness came over him. He raised

[8] sound made by chewing food,
G. zermalmen
[9] ate hurriedly and noisily
[10] [ˈfjuːdʒitivz]

[11] [huˈrei]

[12] moved

[13] deed
[14] frighten

5* Modern English (4106)

his poor shamed eyes to the sun, a great sob shook him, he shuddered twice and then lay still.

So passed from the earth, jeered at¹⁵, mocked and insulted, the last of all the dragons.

(abridged)

circ. 539 words

An Adventure under the Sea

¹ laughed

"Hello!" chuckled¹ George as I came along with a towel round my neck and a wet costume in my hand; "been swimming round the Dodman?"

² high land jutting out into the sea, G. Vorgebirge

The Dodman was a tall headland² a mile or more away, and so I only laughed. "But I have been diving too," I said.

"Did you get right to the bottom?" asked George.

"I did once," I replied.

³ [ˈneptjuːn]

"You did not meet Father Neptune³, I suppose?" he said.

I shook my head. "I wouldn't have seen him if I had," I replied, "for I can't open my eyes underwater."

"I did some diving once," went on George, "and I got the fright of my life. If I told you it would frighten you so much that you'd cry."

"Don't be silly, George!" I said; "how could I be frightened when I'm sitting here with you in the sunshine. *Do* tell me."

"Good for you," grinned George. "Now listen. It was real diving in a diver's suit, you know, and not just ducking under and up again like a sea-gull."

⁴ rescue of property from loss at sea, G. Bergungs-
⁵ [tɔːˈpiːdoud]

"It was just after the war, and I was the chief diver on the salvage⁴ ship 'Rodney'. A liner had been torpedoed⁵ and sunk just off the south-west coast of Ireland during the war, and we were going to raise her."

⁶ sharply pulled

"I was in charge of one of the boats from which the divers went down. A diver, Harry Smith, was the first one to go down one morning. Suddenly his signal rope began to be jerked⁶ violently. As quickly as possible we

68

pulled him up and had him into the boat. As soon as his helmet was off we saw that something was wrong with him. He could not speak for a while, but at last he said, 'There's a ghost down there in that ship, and it's the ghost of a diver!' "

"I laughed aloud. 'Don't be a fool, Harry,' I said. 'You know very well that ghosts are only a tale to frighten silly people with.' "

" 'I don't care what you say,' mumbled[7] Harry; 'but I know what I saw.' "

" 'You're daft[8], man,' I said. 'Here, I'll go down; where did you see this bogey?' "[9]

" 'In the saloon,' he replied; 'and if you take my advice you'll stay where you are.' "

"But by this time I was half-way down the little rope-ladder over the stern[10], and they were screwing on my helmet. And in another ten minutes I was on the bottom of the sea. I made my way to the saloon of the sunken liner and stared round. And then I gasped inside my helmet and felt my heart thump like a hammer. There, sure enough, not a dozen paces ahead of me was another diver, and a queer, big, ghostly sort of chap he was. I drew my knife and moved forward. And then I laughed aloud in my helmet. The whole of one end of the saloon was a big looking-glass, and the ghostly diver was my own reflection!

"And," ended George with a chuckle, "you'll find that all ghost stories have just such a simple explanation if only you trouble to look for it."   (abridged)

[7] murmured

[8] foolish, crazy
[9] also bogy = devil, G. Kobold

[10] ship's hinder end, G. Heck

A Queer Wreck*

"Have you ever been wrecked?" I asked George when I met him on the beach.

"Wrecked?" said George. Presently he smiled and then laughed aloud. "I was once wrecked by a rice-pudding!" he said.

circ. 431 words
* [rek]

"By a what!" I cried.

"By a rice-pudding!" repeated George.

"Don't be silly!" I laughed. "How could a rice-pudding wreck a ship?"

"Listen, and you'll learn," replied George.

"It was like this. About twenty-five years ago it must be. I was on the 'Southern Queen', a fine four-masted barque[1] that did the voyage to India and back twice a year, no matter what the weather was. She had been a fine ship in her young days, but she was old then, and more fit to be broken up than to meet the storms and monsoons of the Indian Ocean.

"Well, we left Bombay one April morning with a cargo of rice.

"We had bad luck from the start. The first day one of the hands slipped and broke his leg; and the next day Slushy, the cook, scalded[2] his leg so badly that he was in his bunk[3] for a week.

"It was the middle of the second week that we struck our first bad gale. The old ship *stood up to*[4] it pretty well, but the hammering she got from the heavy seas strained[5] her planks so badly that she began to leak[6]; and from then onward until we were wrecked we were at the pumps.

"We seemed to be always pumping; and even when we slept we pumped in our dreams.

"But pump as we did the water still came in. That wouldn't have mattered much if we'd had any other cargo but rice. Put a handful of rice in water and it swells as big as a football. Well, that's what happened to our cargo. Why, we could feel it swelling[7] under our feet. And the way the planks of the poor old 'Southern Queen' creaked and groaned under the strain was frightful to hear.

"The captain was a pigheaded[8] old man and wouldn't put into port anywhere. He said we'd reach home safe enough. Well, we *did*—but not in the 'Southern Queen'. We were half-way across the Bay of Biscay[9] when the old ship let out a crack like a smack[10] of thunder. She opened

1 also bark = vessel

2 injured with hot liquid, G. verbrühen
3 sleeping-berth, G. (Schlaf=) Koje
4 G. setzte sich zur Wehr gegen
5 pulled at
6 let water pass

7 grow bigger

8 obstinate, G. dickköpfig

9 ['biskei]
10 blow

70

out like a burst barrel, and we'd only time to tumble into the boats before she went down. Luckily the sea was fairly calm and we were picked up before nightfall. And that," ended George with a chuckle[11], "is how I was wrecked by a rice-pudding!"

(abridged)

[11] quiet laugh

The Peewit's* Storm

circ. 316 words
* also pewit ['piːwit]
= lapwing,
G. Kiebitz

With almost unfailing regularity every April, there occurs in Scotland and the mountains of the north of England what we call the Peewit's Storm, with snow and gale. It often follows lovely spring days, and it is called the Peewit's Storm because it occurs when the peewits are just beginning to nest.

I well remember being caught in the Peewit's Storm when a boy. I was high in the hills when I saw the storm approaching across the glen[1]. The sun was shining where I stood, but it was just as though a great black curtain was being dragged[2] across the valley, and beyond it one could see nothing. I made for the nearest stone wall, realizing that if I followed the wall, it would not only give me some shelter, but would lead me down to the valley.

Just as I reached the wall the storm reached me, and at once I realized how it is that people become dazed[3] and helpless when caught thus. It was like falling into a river of icy water, for the cold went straight through one's clothes, and one could not lift one's face to the fury[4] of it. It was like a furious sandstorm, blinding one's face, so that there was nothing for it but to crouch[5] and pray that it would soon be over. When it died down a little I started to follow the wall down to the valley, knowing that they would be anxious at home, but as luck would have it I actually stumbled over a shepherd I knew, who was crouching in the shelter. He told me that we had nothing to fear, as he had his dog with him, and

[1] narrow valley, G. Bergschlucht

[2] drawn along

[3] stupefied bewildered

[4] wild anger
[5] bend timidly, G. sich ducken

71

a good sheep dog will always take you safely home. So when the first of the storm was ended we tied a string to the dog's collar, and he faithfully led us to safety.

(abridged)

QUELLENNACHWEIS

1. The Monkey's Story (The Jewel in the Monkey's Heart), in: "Story Time in the Zoo", by R. K. and M. I. R. Polkinghorne; Longmans, Green and Co Ltd, London 1960, ... pp. 32—42.

2. The Rabbit's Story (The Clever One outwitted), in: "Story Time in the Zoo", by R. K. and M. I. R. Polkinghorne; Longmans, Green and Co Ltd, London 1960, ... pp. 133—142.

3. The Old Stag, in: "Wild Animals at Home", by H. Mortimer Batten; Longmans, Green and Co Ltd, London 1948, ... pp. 53—59.

4. The Sea-Lion's Story (Pomara, the Sea-Lion's Friend), in: "Story Time in the Zoo", by R. K. and M. I. R. Polkinghorne; Longmans, Green and Co Ltd, London 1960, ... pp. 94—105.

5. The Elephant's Stories (1. The Kind-Hearted Elephant), in: "Story Time in the Zoo", by R. K. and M. I. R. Polkinghorne; Longmans, Green and Co Ltd, London 1960, ... pp. 43—48.

6. Down below and up above, in: "Tell me another", by Stephen Southwold; Longmans, Green and Co Ltd, London 1961, ... pp. 14—17.

7. The Coyote's Story (Why the Coyote has Yellow Eyes), in: "Story Time in the Zoo", by R. K. and M. I. R. Polkinghorne; Longmans, Green and Co Ltd, London 1960, ... pp. 143—150.

8. The Zebu's Story (The Strong Ox), in: "Story Time in the Zoo", by R. K. and M. I. R. Polkinghorne; Longmans, Green and Co Ltd, London 1960, ... pp. 78—82.

9. The Bear's Story (The Young Bears and their Troubles), in: "Story Time in the Zoo", by R. K. and M. I. R. Polkinghorne; Longmans, Green and Co Ltd, London 1960, ... pp. 3—15.

10. The Crafty Sprat, in: "Tell me another", by Stephen Southwold; Longmans, Green and Co Ltd, London 1961, ... pp. 48—51.

11. The Story of the Fox (The Clever Fox), in: "Story Time in the Zoo", by R. K. and M. I. R. Polkinghorne; Longmans, Green and Co Ltd, London 1960, ... pp. 61—67.

12. The Stork and the Heron, in: "Story Time in time in the Zoo", by R. K. and M. I. R. Polkinghorne; Longmans, Green and Co Ltd, London 1948 pp. 73—77.

13. The Lion's Story (The Three Cubs), in: "Story Time in the Zoo", by R. K. and M. I. R. Polkinghorne; Longmans, Green and Co Ltd, London 1960, ... pp. 170—174.

14. The Biter Bitten, in: "Tell me another", by Stephen Southwold; Longmans, Green and Co Ltd, London 1961, ... pp. 52—59.

15. The Parrot's Story (Polly flies away from home), in: "Story Time in the Zoo", by R. K. and M. I. R. Polkinghorne; Longmans, Green and Co Ltd, London 1960, ... pp. 84—93.

16. The Camel's Story (The Ugly Wise One), in: "Story Time in the Zoo", by R. K. and M. I. R. Polkinghorne; Longmans, Green and Co Ltd, London 1960, ... pp. 160—169.

17. The Jackal's Story (The Blue Jackal), in: "Story Time in the Zoo", by R. K. and M. I. R. Polkinghorne; Longmans, Green and Co Ltd, London 1960, ... pp. 68—72.

18. The Sparrow and the Weathercock, in: "Tell me another", by Stephen Southwold; Longmans, Green and Co Ltd, London 1961, ... pp. 18—21.

19. The Cavy's Story (How the Owls of the Pampas treated their Friends), in: "Story Time in the Zoo", by R. K. and M. I. R. Polkinghorne; Longmans, Green and Co Ltd, London 1960, ... pp. 151—159.

20. For One Day only, in: "Tell me another", by Stephen Southwold; Longmans, Green and Co Ltd, London 1961, ... pp. 128—130.

21. The Conceited Fly, in: "Tell me another", by Stephen Southwold; Longmans, Green and Co Ltd, London 1961, ... pp. 11—13.

22. The Clock-Work-Mouse's Tale, in: "Tell me another", by Stephen Southwold; Longmans, Green and Co Ltd, London 1961, ... pp. 44—47.

23. The Stork, in: "Tell me another", by Stephen Southwold; Longmans, Green and Co Ltd, London 1961, ... pp. 8—10.

24. Grey Lag the Leader, in: "Wild Animals at Home", by H. Mortimer Batten; Longmans, Green and Co Ltd, London 1948, ... pp. 21—27.

25. A Lucky Scare or the Story how a Dish came into Existence, in: "Tell me another", by Stephen Southwold; Longmans, Green and Co Ltd, London 1961, ... pp. 28—35.

26. Federigo's Falcon, in: "A Heritage of Wonder Stories", by John H. Walsh and Alice M. Walsh; Longmans, Green and Co Ltd, London 1964, pp. 90—94.

27. The Wonderful Ingredient, in: "Tell me another", by Stephen Southwold; Longmans, Green and Co Ltd, London 1961, ... pp. 60—69.

28. The Hat, in: "Tell me another", by Stephen Southwold; Longmans, Green and Co Ltd, London 1961, ... pp. 22—27.

29. The King's Pimple, in: "Tell me another", by Stephen Southwold; Longmans, Green and Co Ltd, London 1961, ... pp. 79—87.

30. The Cat, in: "Tell me another", by Stephen Southwold; Longmans, Green and Co Ltd, London 1961, ... pp. 88—91.

31. The Old Tin Soldier, in: "Tell me another", by Stephen Southwold; Longmans, Green and Co Ltd, London 1961, ... pp. 98—101.

32. The Story of the Tortoise (How the Tortoise came to have a Shell), in: "Story Time in the Zoo", by R. K. and M. I. R. Polkinghorne; Longmans Green and Co Ltd, London 1960, ... pp. 16—21.

33. The Shop on the Beach, in: "Tell me another", by Stephen Southwold; Longmans, Green and Co Ltd, London 1961, ... pp. 164—173.

34. Limpy Peter's Pet, in: "Tell me another", by Stephen Southwold; Longmans, Green and Co Ltd, London 1961, ... pp. 160—163.

35. Dibble's Garden, in: "Tell me another", by Stephen Southwold; Longmans, Green and Co Ltd, London 1961, ... pp. 179—185.

36. The Swan, in: "Tell me another", by Stephen Southwold; Longmans, Green and Co Ltd, London 1961, ... pp. 121—127.

37. The "Elizabeth Kilner", in: "Tell me another", by Stephen Southwold; Longmans, Green and Co Ltd, London, ... pp. 153—159.

38. The Cry in the Fog, in: "Tell me another", by Stephen Southwold; Longmans, Green and Co Ltd, London 1961, ... pp. 174—178.

39. The Last Dragon, in: "Tell me another", by Stephen Southwold; Longmans, Green and Co Ltd, London 1961, ... pp. 106—113.

40. An Adventure under the Sea, in: "Tell me another", by Stephen Southwold; Longmans, Green and Co Ltd, London 1961, ... pp. 40—43.

41. A Queer Wreck, in: "Tell me another", by Stephen Southwold; Longmans, Green and Co Ltd, London 1961, ... pp. 36—39.

42. The Peewit's Storm, in: "Wild Animals at Home", by H. Mortimer Batten; Longmans, Green and Co Ltd, London 1948, ... pp. 119—124.

Aids to Modern English

Diesterwegs Neusprachliche Arbeitsmittel

Ab 4. Lehrjahr   MD-Nr.

Crowell jr., A Glossary of Phrases with Prepositions.
VII, 216 S.   (4102)
Fuchs, Englische Nacherzählungen für die Mittelstufe. 75 S.   (4106)
Hill, Exercises for Senior Pupils. 108 S.   (4109)
Roller, Anecdotes About Famous British People. 132 S.   (4114)

Oberstufe
English and German Style
Ein Arbeitsheft für den Englischunterricht mit englischen und
deutschen Originaltexten nebst Übertragungen und einem stil-
kundlichen Anhang. Hrsg. von K. Schrey, 61 S.   (4090)
Listen and Retell. Englische Nacherzählungen für die Oberstufe
der Höheren Schule. Hrsg. von P. Riegel. 64 S.   (4092)
Englische Diktattexte für die Oberstufe. Von W. Fischer. 80 S.   (4096)
Neue englische Texte für die Oberstufe der Höheren Schule.
Erste Folge: **Great Britain.** Hrsg. von G. Burkholz. 104 S.   (4097)
Zweite Folge: **die USA.** Hrsg. von G. Burkholz. 108 S.   (4107)
Englische Nacherzählungstexte für die Reifeprüfung
Hrsg. von K. Fuchs. 116 S.   (4100)
How to Avoid Mistakes
Ein Lernbuch für die Oberstufe. Aussprache, Schreibung, Wort-
wahl, Grammatik. Von H. Brinkmann. VIII, 148 S.   (4101)
Stilkunde des Englischen. Von K. Wittig
Arbeitsheft für den Schüler. VI, 150 S.   (4103)
Handbuch für den Lehrer
(aus der Reihe „Schule und Forschung"). 258 S.   (4207)
Problems and Opinions
A Selection of British and American Texts with Comprehension
and Discussion Exercises. Bearbeitet und hrsg. von G. Kostuch. 120 S. (4104)
Die englische Herübersetzung in der Schule
Hilfen zur Übersetzung Englisch-Deutsch
Ein Arbeits- und Lernbuch für die Oberstufe zur Vermeidung
von Fehlern. Von W. Fischer. 47 S.   (4111)
Science in the Modern World. Von W. Mäcking und G. Penkwitt   (4115)
Modern English Texts for Comprehension and Analysis
Hrsg. von E. Sörensen   (4116)
English Texts Compared. Hrsg. von A.-R. Glaap   (4117)
Scientific Readings in English. Hrsg. von H. R. Matthäi.   (4118)

Diesterweg

403/1